DESIGN THE HOME
YOU LOVE

DESIGN THE HOME YOU LOVE

PRACTICAL STYLING ADVICE TO MAKE THE MOST OF YOUR SPACE

LEE MAYER WITH EMILY MOTAYED
FOUNDERS OF HAVENLY

IN COLLABORATION WITH HEATHER GOERZEN

TEN SPEED PRESS
California | New York

TABLE OF CONTENTS

INTRODUCTION

Design can be hard. Design can be intimidating. Design, frankly, can even be scary sometimes. For so many of us, matching paint colors and choosing the right sofa for our spaces is not exactly intuitive.

To make matters worse, when you enter into the design world, it feels so rarified—fancy designers talking about incredibly beautiful but oh-so-expensive objets d'art that feel as if they would never survive life with two toddler boys and a dog. We knew that if the two of us were feeling in need of more accessible professional design help, there must be hundreds, if not thousands, of other people who felt the same way.

On top of it all, in these HGTV-obsessed days, we are constantly bombarded by images of perfect rooms. (Where *do* they hide their electric cords, seriously?) If you're anything like Emily and me, you're feeling a little bit like you can't compete. We have lives, jobs, bills, pets, maybe even kids, and getting your home Instagram-perfect can often be the last priority.

Havenly is the company we started in 2014 to help make designing and decorating your home easier. We had both moved, both felt like we were at turning points in our lives (Lee had just gotten married; Emily had just gotten her first job), but both of us felt it took us a long time to get our new places furnished. We were both working full-time, and while we really wanted our homes to reflect our personalities, we just didn't have the time to pore over hundreds of websites to find the exact right items—items that all went together *and* that were in our price range.

Our inability to put our homes together created a lot of stress. Lee remembers coming home late from a long workday, sitting on the floor of her empty living room, and trying to figure out which sofa and rugs she should buy. She was paralyzed by all the decisions she needed to make, and she felt as if her vision for a perfectly executed dinner party was moving further and further away.

As we went through this experience, we both felt as if something was missing in the home-design space. In our experience, there was no way that a normal, I-don't-have-a-$200K-budget-for-furniture-are-you-kidding-me? gal could easily navigate through the many expensive options in the furniture market and end up with a beautifully and affordably designed, but still livable, home. We wanted to create a welcoming community where we made design dreams come true, without any judgment or pretense.

We saw that the traditional interior design model—you know, the one where someone fancy comes into your home and holds your hand through the entire design process—was cost prohibitive for many people. (I mean, honestly, for $300 an hour, shouldn't we get a designed home *as well as* our dinner made and the kids put to bed?) On the other hand, we learned how overwhelming it can be to undertake a design project on your own. Let's be honest: for the slightly less home-decor inclined, Pinterest ideas in execution can end up looking more like science projects gone wrong, and the time investment to get it all done is something that so many of us can't afford in our busy lives.

The hard part, for us at least, was making the leap from lucrative traditional careers into starting a company around design. We realized though, as we talked to hundreds of friends, colleagues, and family members, that we weren't the only ones feeling bewildered at the prospect of designing a well-presented home. Clearly a market existed, and ultimately, the risk of leaving our careers to pursue an idea that we felt had a lot of people excited wasn't as big as the potential regret of missing an opportunity to help a lot of people like us.

And so . . . we created Havenly.

Our mission with Havenly is to make design accessible to everyone. Because don't we all deserve a beautiful home? We believed that technology could help deliver design services cheaper and more easily no matter where in the country you live, and so we set off to start an online design company. Fast-forward several years, and we are proud to have built a company that is providing work for hundreds of people, has raised nearly $60 million in venture capital, and has created more than one million designs across the country. It feels as if we have come a long way!

We didn't start out as designers. But in the course of helping all of our customers and sorting through all of the data that we have on what people like and don't like and what they need in their homes, we have learned a lot of tips and tricks that we are excited to share with you. So get prepared as we think through how to get started, your budget, your colors, the different styles you can choose from, and how to actually make your home dreams become a reality.

Here's the deal: we know there's a ton of home decor information out there, and every day you're being bombarded with blogs and photos and maybe even TV shows that boast about "Transformations on a Budget!" or "Celebrities Homes and How to Re-Create Them!" But do you ever feel that after reading everything that's out there, the information overload just leads to paralysis, leaving you staring at your unadorned walls or confused about which sofa that will work best for your living room? Or maybe you feel that some of the information that's out there isn't really relevant to your style, budget, and taste, so you feel at a loss for how to incorporate those tips into your personal space.

That's where we come in. We've created this book, *Design the Home You Love*, with a completely fresh approach to designing a home that's curated from the best design advice we've learned. We have created a way to break down the ambiguous and sometimes intimidating world of home decor, to help you start your own home journey armed with information and education, and to set out the defining qualities that make for a beautiful home—for all styles and budgets. In becoming one of the country's leading online design firms, we have worked with hundreds of thousands of clients, and from that experience, we have created a proprietary framework that is data driven, but can be personalized to your needs. Throughout this book, Lee will lead you through her journey and a lot of the basics and interior designer–approved tricks to creating a home that is uniquely you and that works for you and your family. Emily will be adding in real-world solutions to some design dilemmas that she's faced and she's seen clients face along the way. We hope you enjoy the ride.

xo, Lee and Emily

LEE'S STORY

I came to interior design in a funny way. I grew up in the suburbs of
Washington, DC, as the child of Indian immigrants. My parents were delighted
to give us a lot of opportunity, but, at the same time, they emphasized
the importance of education, a common theme among the parents of first-
generation south Asian children. It was our parents' focus and dedication
that led me to Columbia University for my undergraduate degree and later to
Harvard Business School for my MBA. However, their dedication to education
underlay a desire for us to pursue stable careers, ones that came with large
paychecks and a path to a corner office. I internalized a lot of their dreams,
and initially pursued very traditional paths for work, spending time in finance,
corporate development, and management consulting. These jobs surrounded
me with incredibly intelligent people but didn't encourage me to pursue
business in a more creative space . . . or build anything new.

So why design? I think both Emily and I have always been enchanted with
the idea of home and the role it can play in one's life. I remember how much
time I spent in my family home and how central the idea of home was to
my family. I remember learning multiplication tables at our kitchen counter,
creating bedsheet forts in our hallway, and learning how to make my bed in
my first big-kid bedroom. Beyond that, my mom always invested in making
our family home feel personal to her. She enjoyed entertaining in her home,

throwing large parties and decorating her home to entertain. I have these incredible memories of going to an exhausting series of furniture stores with my mother as she bought her first new sofa when our family could finally afford a larger home. Even today, my mom spends time collecting for her home; her formal living room, for example, is decorated with curios and figurines from her travels around the world. For us, our home was not just the center of our family life; it was a reflection of who we were and what we loved to do.

As I left for college, I realized that home continued to be critical to my overall happiness. I moved from Washington D.C. to New York City and, as so many college freshmen do, moved into a cramped and shared dorm room. It didn't take long for me to realize how unsettled I felt living in a place where I didn't feel at home. I set to work fixing that, convincing my (extremely tolerant) roommate, Lauren, to cover the peeling linoleum floors with an area rug, and finding (regrettably mass printed and generic—*Starry Night*, anyone?) art to pretty up the painted cinderblock walls. It wasn't perfect, but our room was in my opinion, the most comfortable dorm room on Carman 11, and I loved coming home after a long day of classes (and—let's be honest—all too often, a long night of college parties) to a place that felt more like home.

While I clearly appreciated the magic of a well-designed space, I didn't really think about design much from a professional standpoint. That changed when I landed in Denver after nearly twelve years of New York City living. All of a sudden, I owned a home—one with multiple bedrooms and a real kitchen (with a dishwasher, praise be!). And that's when I really started to understand this need for a more accessible entry point for interior design help, and my professional career took a little bit of a left turn as Emily and I started Havenly.

We realized there had to be a way to connect designers with customers and potentially make the process easier and more affordable by bringing it online. With that initial idea, we kicked off this crazy journey that led to Havenly. It took a lot of dedication, a pinch of creativity, and a little (okay, a lot of) help from our friends until we were able to turn that original idea into a company that's transformed hundreds of thousands of clients' spaces that were uniquely personal to them.

Over the course of the last six years, we have seen it all and been through more. We've helped people decorate their first apartments, followed them through to their first home purchases, and helped them adapt to growing families. We have built a team of hundreds, all committed to our mission of democratizing interior design and creating a design community for everyone—no matter your individual style, taste, or budget.

Ultimately, Havenly is made up of a group of hardworking women and men who understand the value of a beautiful home and the effect that it can have on overall productivity, satisfaction, and happiness, especially for those who appreciate the value of stretching each dollar as far as it can go. We wanted Havenly to embody those principles because we embody them as individuals in real life—that you don't have to spend a fortune to make your home feel like a home, and you shouldn't feel bad about having to stick to a budget.

PART I

THE FOUNDATION

YOU HAVE A HOME. YOU EVEN HAVE PINTEREST BOARDS. NOW WHAT?

There are so many ways to think about starting your project, and we know it probably feels overwhelming. At Havenly, we feel that it's helpful to start by asking this fundamental question of our clients: *Where are you on your home journey?* To be more specific: *Are you starting from scratch? Are you just looking to spruce up an existing room or two? Are you just looking for a few specific items?*

Once you understand your starting point, we typically ask about your budget. After having worked with so many clients, we have found that a lot of us aren't well equipped to know what our budget should be. Are you unsure about which items in your room are great investment candidates, and which areas are prime candidates for a bargain deal? Well, we'll help you figure that out. We know that sometimes decorating a whole new place isn't the most fun thing for your wallet, but making an investment in the right items can actually be a way to create future returns. Not to mention, you'll be creating a space that makes you comfortable and feels like you. Can you even put a price on that?

We aren't saying you have to spend a fortune to achieve your perfect home, but it does make sense to be realistic about what you'll need to save up to create the home of your dreams. Just think: giving up your daily Starbucks lattes for a month or two, or forgoing that dress you'll really wear only once can result in a space that you'll create memories in for years to come.

Just picture the book club meetings, the home-cooked meals with generous pours of a lovely Cabernet, the late-night bonding sessions with your spouse or friends, the summer barbecues. I'm not saying that having a home that reflects you will make your life Gwyneth Paltrow–style perfect, but I'm not *not* saying it either.

We're getting ahead of ourselves, so let's begin with that fundamental question: *Where are you on your home journey?*

WHICH OF THE FOLLOWING DESCRIPTIONS BEST FITS YOUR SITUATION?

A. You are in a totally blank-space state of mind. You're going to start from scratch and are ready for a total transformation.

B. You're not sure what to think. You have a look or feel in mind, but you're not sure what to keep and what to toss in order to achieve that feeling you're craving in your space.

C. You've got the big stuff. You're pretty sure you love your couch/art/rug/coffee table, but now you need to bring it to life with some personality.

D. Everything is fine, but you're in the mood to change it up a little, and aren't sure which direction to go.

HERE ARE OUR FIVE RULES TO SET THE STAGE FOR YOUR REDECORATION:

1. Come up with a budget so you can figure out where to splurge and where to save.

2. Avoid the shortcuts that may eventually be costly.

3. Think about proportion and scale when choosing your items.

4. Lighting design is your friend; layer for best effect.

5. Color is the key to a cohesive and interesting look.

Our goal throughout this chapter is to help you with the foundational elements. We want you to audit your space, get a sense of your budget, and then learn a little bit about color theory and how proportions and space planning combine to get you a perfectly designed, finished-looking home.

Let's embark upon our design journey with an audit of your space. The easiest way to get started is to walk through each room that you're considering in need of some love. We'll walk through the items you need and give you some tips on how to think about selecting the right items. We'll also talk about where to spend and where to save. One word of warning: we will have opinions, and they've come from helping a lot of people find their own style. However, your home is for YOU and only YOU! If some of our advice doesn't serve you or your family and lifestyle, then ignore it! The only rule in design is that there are no real rules.

AUDITING YOUR SPACE

LIVING ROOM

I had just moved into an older home with Jason, my husband, and his two adorable but rambunctious boys, Carter and Grayson, who at the time were five and two. All of a sudden the perfectly functional but slightly small living room felt completely impractical for our new combined lives. I dreaded coming home to the toy cars that were inevitably scattered over the rug and the multiple sippy cups resting precariously on our accent chairs. Carter, our toddler, kept running into the sharp edges of the coffee table, and there was no space for either of the kids to play. Sure, the room was on the smaller side, which I really couldn't change, but one of the things I realized was that the individual items in the room were ill-suited to our young family's lifestyle.

So we replaced our sofa and chairs with a more functional and space-saving sectional in a light gray pebble weave (the texture of the fabric was chosen to hide handprints and the dirt that little boys seem to be magnets for), and we built large covered storage bins for toys. We also found a better-proportioned coffee table that left more room for impromptu games of catch but that didn't have sharp edges as our youngest found his walking legs. Suddenly, what once felt cluttered and messy became a safe haven—a place where everyone loved to congregate and that had plenty of functionality for our growing family.

Unsurprisingly, the living room is the room most people seek help for at Havenly. Is any other place in your house as representative of your life? This is where your family and friends will gather for family game night; it's where you'll kick up your feet at the end of a long day (with wine and Netflix, naturally). This is also the room that made us so passionate about starting Havenly. When I moved into my first real home a few years ago, I had no idea how to think about this central of a space, so I sought help to understand how and where to invest in pieces for the living room.

I've learned a lot about designing this space, and at Havenly we've seen many successful designs transform a living room. We think we have unique ways for you to think about both your items and how to budget for this all-important room. Let's walk through the most common things we look for in a well-composed living room so you can understand what to think about buying, how to assess what you already have, and what to invest in.

We'll suggest where to "Splurge" or where you might want to consider spending a little bit more for a higher-quality investment item. We'll also identify items on which you may want to "Save" and really optimize for a good deal. There are also some areas where the decision is really up to how much you value the added quality of a splurge for that particular item.

SOFA / SPLURGE

The grounding element for every living room is the main seating piece. Pretty much every living room will need a functional but attractive sofa. This is also often the most expensive investment in your living or family room, and in our opinion, it should be. After all, it's the space that you're using the most, and, given the way most of us live today, the living room often has to serve a lot of purposes. The sofa grounds your living area and provides a lot of the basis for the look and feel of the room. However, the sofa also has to be super functional and comfortable—after all, we spend a lot of time hanging out on it. In talking to our clients, we find that many people use their sofa as a dining room, play area, nap room, and gathering place. That's what makes the sofa decision a hard one; it's a piece that has to hold up not only from a style perspective but also from a performance perspective. In 2020, as my sofa became not just my place to relax after a long day of work but also my workstation and where the kids were home schooled, I rediscovered the importance of having a beautiful but comfortable sofa. I was so relieved that my investment sectional held up really well under the added wear and tear, and it became the piece of furniture that I was most grateful to have spent a little extra to get right.

Do you have a sofa but aren't sure whether to keep it?

Here's a tip: DON'T hold onto a sofa that isn't pretty awesome. I'm telling you: your living room will never look the way you want it to if you keep an old, tired, and uninspired sofa—no matter how much you think about the other accessories in your living room. On top of that, you'll never feel at home if you hold onto a damaged or uncomfortable sofa. If you're not looking forward to sitting on it, it's not worth having. In some cases, particularly now that you can get sofas for less than $700, a new sofa can actually SAVE you money—by being the one thing you need to totally upgrade your look.

Consider getting a new sofa if your current sofa

is overstuffed

is made of faux black leather

is both overstuffed and faux black leather

is in possession of overly curvy arms

is covered in cheap microfiber

has too much going on (multiple fabrics or patterns or too many nailhead details)

is any or all of the above.

In short, if you don't love your sofa, you should definitely consider getting a new one. These dated looks won't make your living room modern and clean because the sofa is such a core component of your room. If you keep your old sofa and then, to remedy the room's look, you spend money on other things, you'll still be disappointed with the result.

What happens if you have a sofa that you absolutely love that fits one of the descriptors on the "don't keep" list above? That's okay, too. In our opinion, rules are meant to be broken when it comes to decorating a home that's wonderfully you. Really, we won't be mad at you, as long as your sofa fits the look you are going for. You have our blessing to work with whatever you have that you really, really love. Our only advice is that if you're having any

A SOFA WE LOVE

JASPER SOFA, INTERIOR DEFINE

We love the clean lines of this sofa. We also love that it is available as a sectional (which I have!) and comes in fabrics that are customizable and can be kid and pet friendly.

sort of doubts around either the form or function of the sofa, you truly should consider a new investment. As you think about your budget, you're more likely to have a higher level of satisfaction per dollar if you ensure that your sofa is up to your tastes. You'll thank me later. After all, friends don't let friends have ugly sofas—and we're friends, right?

Remember, just because you need to get a new sofa doesn't mean you have to spend a fortune. While I certainly recommend spending as much on this key element as possible, if you're in a spot where you don't have a big budget for any item on your list, with a little bit of luck, and patience, you can get great deals by scouring Craigslist or other vintage marketplaces.

Keep your sofa if it's clean and functional and doesn't remind you of the nineties (a particularly bad time for sofas, we think). Try to find one that doesn't have legs that are too heavy and has clean lines that can be versatile and fit different styles. As we look at what is sold most often in this category, we find that most clients really love sofas that have a neutral color base (think shades of gray, cream, or blue) with modern but durable construction.

Another thing to consider is how the sofa fits into the space—and by the way, get used to us talking about fit and proportion; it's the easiest way to convey a put-together decor look. But proportion is doubly important for an element as foundational to your room as the sofa. As the dominant item, usually, in your living room, your sofa needs to be neither too small nor too large. We'll talk about space planning in a later chapter, but we find that most people have good intuition about what works from a space perspective.

If you have a large living room and you're worried that your sofa is too small, consider adding a second facing sofa or a set of chairs, either of which may provide you with enough seating and fullness to create a comfortable but well-proportioned space. Or, consider a sectional for extra dimension and comfort. I'm a sectional fan myself, and in our large great room, I have both a right-facing sectional and a pair of chairs. It ensures that I have spots for a lot of guests when I'm entertaining, but also enough room to put my feet up and watch TV at the end of a long day.

On the other hand, if you are in a smaller space, you do want to be careful not to choose a sofa that is too big or overwhelming. Too much sofa can make a space feel cramped and crowded, and you'd be better served by providing accent seating (or modular seating) paired with a smaller-scale sofa to allow for easy movement through the room, while offering enough seating for your guests. In very small apartments, I've even seen people make good use of seating alternatives: a love seat, a day bed, or even four chairs can be suitable substitutes for a sofa if they fit the proportions of your small space.

Regardless of size, your sofa should be comfortable, stylish, and a good canvas to showcase parts of your design personality. A few years ago, I'd typically say that sofas under $1500 were impossible to find, unless you were looking at secondhand options. The good news is that you can find some inexpensive options now that are stylish and comfortable—if a little less durable. If you're not looking for a sofa to last for decades, it's no longer impossible to find a sofa under even $700! Wayfair, IKEA, and a few direct-to-consumer retailers like Campaign or Burrow all have stylish and functional options around that price point. Campaign sofas even come in a box, so it's easy to have them delivered.

If you're going the used route, or have a sofa that you think is comfortable but needs an update, here are some tips for making the old new again.

1. Clean it or get it cleaned. Nothing revitalizes a piece of furniture like a good deep clean and stain removal. If you go to a pro, look for local deals and ensure that your cleaner is familiar with the fabric on your sofa.

2. Consider reupholstery to modernize the look. A professional is probably required here, unless you're up for a DIY project, but recovering can be an inexpensive way to breathe new life into furniture you already own.

3. If reupholstery is too pricey, think about buying a well-fitting slipcover. The key here is to look for a slipcover that isn't overly large or small and has a tailored look to it so that you don't risk the sofa looking sloppy.

4. Think about refinishing legs and accents. If you have dark wood legs that don't suit the rest of your color scheme, sand off the finish and restain. You can also add or remove nailhead trim and many other details as well.

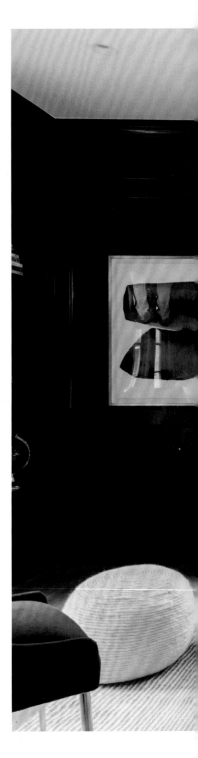

LET'S TALK ABOUT A FEW DIFFERENT TYPES OF SOFAS THAT YOU MIGHT FIND ON THE MARKET:

THE MID-CENTURY MODERN SOFA

For many years, the mid-century modern sofa ruled the conversation with its rectangular shape, clean leg style, and tight seat back. Mid-century modern sofas often feature bolder colors, in shades of blue or orange. If you like the idea of bringing some color and vibrancy into your space, this is a great option for you.

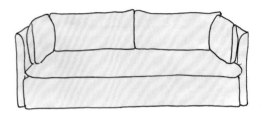

THE CONTEMPORARY SOFA

I think the term *contemporary* is a confusing one, as most people have very different perspectives on what that word means. What's more, the definition will inevitably change, as it is just a word that indicates what is popular at the moment. These days that means simple shapes, unfussy cushions (think bench cushions or two cushions), and classic, but low, arm styles.

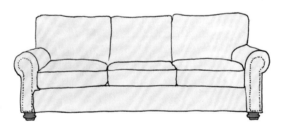

TRADITIONAL SOFAS (ENGLISH THREE-SEATERS OR ROLL-ARM SOFAS)

These classic babies have been on the market for a lot of years and are some of the most common that you will see in your local furniture store. Often this sofa will have a slightly rolled back, and rolled arms, with more roundness in its profile than you will see in the two styles above. While this is a truly classic item, keep in mind that this sofa in particular does imbue your space with a more traditional look. If you'd prefer a modern look, but like some traditional details, think about mixing a traditional accent with a more contemporary-shaped sofa— for example, a contemporary sofa with Chesterfield detailing.

VARIATIONS ON SOFA STYLES

CHESTERFIELD

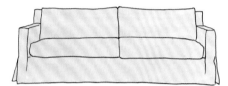

SLIPCOVERED

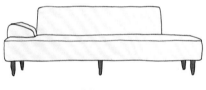

DIVAN

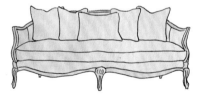

CABRIOLE

LOUIS XV

A SECTIONAL WE LOVE

MELLO TAOS SECTIONAL, ARTICLE

I have this sectional from Article in our TV room, and I love how its oversized look combines with its low profile to give it a modern but comfortable feel. It's great to sink into for movie watching, and the leather is of the variety that looks good with a little bit of wear. It's sort of a lifesaver, because our kids love playing on it, and we all gather on this sectional to relax and hang out.

Don't have a ton of room? Try to avoid going with a loveseat without additional seating. It sounds like a great idea, but most standard-size loveseats (under 5 feet long) accommodate only one person comfortably. Try for a sofa that's at least 6 feet long, and if the sofa is less than 7 feet long, look for one with a single bench cushion, so you can fit three people on it, if necessary, without anyone having to sit in the crack between cushions (which, as we all know is the worst!).

TIPS TO CHOOSE THE PERFECT SOFA

1. SIZE AND SCALE

Think about your intention for the space when choosing a size. Will this be a sofa that you want to sleep on, cozy into, and fill up most of the room? Or do you prefer a more formal seating style with a bit more space? One major consideration to choosing a sofa is inside seat depth, which is the measure from the front of the sofa to the front of the back cushion. Typically, this ranges between 21 and 24 inches. However, if you want to really sink into a sofa, consider a deeper seat—that is at least 24 to 33 inches deep. Sofas with a shallow seat work well for more of a formal space, where the kids aren't crawling all over you to get to the popcorn. Any sofa that has a seat depth that is less than 20 inches deep means that no one will ever really want to sit on it (although it sometimes looks cool and modern).

Don't be afraid to get creative, a plain old sofa-plus-two-chairs arrangement isn't your only option. For example, if you want a sofa that the whole family can sit on for movie night, if you have the space, consider a sectional or a sofa with a chaise, because nothing beats the relaxing feel of putting your feet up while binging on reality TV. These days, you have a lot of modern and sophisticated sectional options to choose from. A sectional is also a great option if you have an open floor plan and want to add some structure to the room or create a separation of living spaces.

There are a few types of sectionals to consider:

L SHAPE

This is the most common type of sectional we see, and it quite literally looks like an L. It can be something like a three-seater option, connected to a two-cushion style. Another similar option is a sofa with a longer chaise.

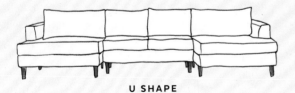

U SHAPE

Another obvious description (it's all in the name, people!), the U shape sofa has two arms on either side of the main sofa that face each other. It gives you lots of space to sit, and also the ability for groups to face each other for easier conversation. If you're choosing a U shape, make sure there's plenty of room to move on either side of the coffee table.

CURVED

To make a statement, consider a curved sectional. This may be a little tricky to do in a smaller space, but if you leave enough room on either side, the curved sectional can be an elegant addition to a living room. Unless you have curved walls, the curved sectional really needs to be placed away from the wall.

2. FABRIC AND COLOR

The question we get asked the most at Havenly is about how furniture will do in the "real world." We have so many clients with dogs/kids/a love of red wine who are so afraid to choose a fabric they love because they fear ruining it. But it's a great time to be alive! The miracle of modern fabrics means that you'll find a lot of incredible materials on the market these days, so you too can have a white or cream sofa without being afraid of little Rover jumping up on it.

Here are some tips and tricks to help make your sofa lifeproof:

- **Look for performance fabrics**: Whether it's Sunbrella's interior line or other performance fabrics offered from your favorite retailers, we've been impressed with the durability of water- and stain-resistant upholstery recently. The best part about these fabrics is that the dirt and wet stuff won't sink in, and usually, if you catch a spill in time, you can just wipe it off, without stains.

- **Make an investment in leather**: A nice, supple leather can go a long way. Great leathers will hide spills, and you can wipe things off quickly. And honestly, a really great leather shines with some wear and tear to add to its character.

- **Protect your upholstery**: We suggest considering a professional coating service if you want to invest in a lighter-color sofa, or generally get longer use out of an upholstered one. There are a number of companies (like Ultraguard) that will help you choose a waterproof coating that increases the likelihood that a sippy cup spill won't stain. We have light sofas all over our house, and we used Ultraguard, so when Carter forgets to take off his shoes after a romp outside, and plops on the couch, we can wipe the residue right off.

- **Pick cleanable options**: Alternatively, choose upholstery that is slipcovered so that you can remove the cover to dry clean it, and choose lighter fabrics that have a little bit of color variation and texture woven into the fabric to hide dirt and stains.

THE TRUTH ABOUT DECORATING IF YOU'RE DEALING WITH A SERIOUSLY LOW BUDGET

Sometimes it's just not the right time to be spending thousands of dollars on anything, let alone home decor. But unfortunately, when it comes to furniture, sticker shock can be a real and very scary thing if you're not approaching design in the right way or looking at the right places. Regardless of what your budget is, rest assured there's a way to create the most perfect haven for you in your home.

Here you'll find all of my tried and true tips for decorating (gathered in consultation with the designers at Havenly). You may think we're a little too optimistic when we say EVERYONE deserves a beautiful home, but we truly mean it, and feel like with just a few inexpensive tweaks, you can really make your space feel fresh.

DECLUTTERING IS YOUR FRIEND

The cheapest and easiest way to instantly upgrade your home is to declutter relentlessly. Get rid of things you don't use, and buy inexpensive drawer organizers and/or shelving from Amazon to put away all of the things that you don't need or use on a daily basis. Keep all visible surfaces neat and clear, and you'll find that your space will look automatically well put-together.

PRO TIP: Detangle and hide your cords. Cord covers are very inexpensive, and if you're working from home or have a lot of gadgets that require electrical cords in your living areas, invest in a few covers to hide those unsightly things. I also think, if you have a standard drywall home, it's worth the investment to pull your TV and cable cords behind the walls. You can get TV cord connectors rather cheaply, and it's usually easy to do.

INVEST WHERE IT MAKES AN IMPACT

As Lee mentioned earlier, if you've even got a small budget, funnel it all into the focal point where it'll be noticed the most. In a living room, that's typically the sofa, and in a bedroom, that's usually the bedframe and duvet combination. It's worth splurging a little (even if it means saving for a few months) to get a focal furniture piece that's both lovely and comfortable. There are so many other places that you can cut corners on price, but the sofa, for example, is very tough to replace. You want to make sure you purchase something that not only is aesthetically pleasing but also is the right type of comfort that you prefer and can last you through the years.

SLIPCOVERS AND THROW PILLOWS CAN HIDE A LOT OF UGLY

However, if a new sofa isn't in the cards for you right now, that's totally okay. Just use some accessories to hide what you're not liking about it. My husband, back when he was my boyfriend, had a dark brown L-shaped sectional in his apartment when I moved in with him, and there was nothing I could do to convince him to get rid of it. Instead, I bought multiple inexpensive but cozy throws and a variety of different throw pillows that were more my speed. Once I threw those on that chocolate-brown sectional, the sofa didn't bother me nearly as much!

Another inexpensive way to hide an ugly sofa is to think about buying a slipcover. You can get relatively simple slipcovers at an affordable price. The key to making a slipcover look good is to make sure that you "zhuzh" it up a little. For example, if there's a bit too much fabric on the arms or in the seat, push the excess fabric down into the creases between the cushions and the frame to help the slipcover stay in its place and look tailored and fitted. You can also use some double-stick tape (or even a grippy rug pad) to help the slipcover stay in place on the back and the seat of the sofa.

FRAME YOUR OWN ART

If we were buying original art, the price tag creeps into the multiple thousands (or millions), but who says art has to be pricey? We don't all need to own our own Kandinsky.

Channel your inner artist by trying your hand at large-scale watercolors and using off-the-shelf frames to dress them up. You can also create a gallery wall with frames from Target of photos that you've taken, either of your family, artistic shots, or a mixture of both types of photos, to create a personalized gallery wall that makes you smile.

If you're not feeling particularly artistic, you can also scout out local art fairs or art programs that often have beautiful pieces for a fraction of the price.

GO SECONDHAND (OR SHOP ONLINE)

There are so many options these days, even beyond Craigslist. Facebook marketplace, LetGo, or Offerup, or even old-fashioned thrifting and antiquing, offer a lot of ability to source and find pre-loved furniture or furnishings. If you're willing to make a quick repair or slap on a coat of paint, you can find real deals that won't break the bank and aren't terribly hard to pull off for the DIY-challenged amongst us (like me!).

Pro tip: Shop sales. Furniture vendors tend to have a pretty consistent sale schedule—Presidents' Day, Memorial Day, July 4th, Labor Day, and Black Friday. They also will typically have a sale in the beginning of the year and midyear to clear out inventory and make space for the new season. Time your purchases well, and you'll be able to get up to 30% off amazing new items, which in turn helps you stay within your budget.

DOUBLE DOWN ON AN ECLECTIC STYLE

I've found that having a little bit of a bohemian or an eclectic style can work very well for people on budgets. This type of intentional mixing allows you to pair a brand-new sofa with a coffee table that you found on a thrift store run. The key here is to keep the look layered, edit obsessively, and ensure that you're consistently eclectic across the space. This allows you to open up your horizons to find great deals while still maintaining a well-put-together home.

To understand how to save on your rug, but still pick the right one, focus on:

PROPORTION

One common mistake we see people make in their living rooms is buying a rug that's too small for the space. So if your rug doesn't fit your space, TOSS IT. (Or better yet and more earth-friendly, repurpose it somewhere else.) I know; it's so tempting to buy a smaller rug—or even keep the smaller rug you already have—as smaller sizes are, after all, less expensive. But we are here to keep you from making mistakes that may save you a little in the short term but will leave you feeling unsatisfied with the finished result.

When rugs are too small, it makes the room feel awkward at best and, at worst, too cold. For most of us with a normal-size living room (unless you live in a shoebox of an apartment like the one I had in the East Village of New York City in 2006) too small likely means any rug less than an 8-foot x 10-foot rug. So think of that as your baseline. A larger living room will do better with a 9-foot x 12-foot rug, and in some cases, you'll need something even larger (I ended up springing for an 11x14 in my great room to get enough coverage). You want the rug to be big enough to have at least two legs of your sofa stand on it (as well as at least two legs of your other furniture pieces, like chairs and

DO THIS

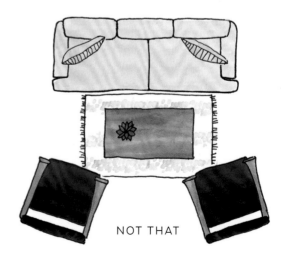

NOT THAT

benches) and also cover the floor substantially. In other words, if you have an 8-foot sofa, you may need a 9-foot x 12-foot rug—you know, so that both legs are on the rug. Yes, that means on the rug, not near the rug or just outside the rug—ON THE RUG. By the way, ideally you have all four furniture legs on the rug, but I know that can sometimes be a high bar.

If you have a small rug that you're thinking about reusing from your previous, smaller home, don't do it unless it really fits the room and the parameters above. If you see a small rug on sale that you think almost covers the space but really doesn't give you the ability to fit your furniture on it, think again. Don't take a shortcut on the size of the rug; you can still save on this item, as long as the rug is big enough for your space. You're putting in the effort to design things; why shortchange your efforts by making everything feel unfinished or, worse, cheap. (Gasp!)

MATERIAL

Apart from those size considerations, save on this item. Rugs sit on the floor, you walk all over them all day, and thankfully, you can find some bargains on the market. A handwoven original Persian carpet is not your only option (although some absolutely beautiful ones do exist). These days you have inexpensive choices ranging from natural jute weaves to flat weaves, and an 8-foot x 10-foot rug can start at just a couple hundred dollars. The best part of saving here is the idea that you can swap out rugs every few years (or even every season, if you're feeling especially creative and have extra money in your budget) and completely change the look of your room.

To best appreciate whether the rug is appropriate for the space, consider the materials. And while you're thinking about the material of your rug, another thing to avoid is a rug that sheds. Kids and pets leave enough detritus on the floor already; your furniture shouldn't add to it, and you don't want to be constantly vacuuming.

WOOL: Probably the most common rug material, wool is durable and soft. Wool also has the benefit of always looking good, even in higher-traffic areas. Wool is stain resistant, and typically, the natural fibers repel dust as well. One thing to know about wool is it can sometimes shed but typically the shedding will lessen over time. Wool rugs can also be a little more expensive, so if wool feels out of your price range, consider cotton or a natural option.

COTTON: A little less expensive than wool, and a great option if you like a flatter style (this means a rug that doesn't have as high of a pile). Cotton rugs are easier to clean than wool rugs but aren't as stain resistant or durable. Cotton flatweave rugs lend a casual air to a space, and so are often used in informal rooms. Because they are inexpensive, cotton rugs are great if you like to change the look of your rug frequently.

NATURAL FIBERS (JUTE, SISAL, BAMBOO): Popular for rooms with a more beachy or coastal vibe. I also think a natural-fiber rug is a great "corrector" if you have a rug that you love that is too small. You can layer a larger jute rug underneath a smaller wool or woven rug to create a properly sized floor covering, for example. These rugs aren't great when wet, and can be hard to remove dirt from, so make sure you put them in an appropriate area.

SILK: If you're craving the soft single-color rugs with a little bit of sheen that you've seen in glam-style living rooms, you may be looking for a silk rug. They look and feel luxurious, and while they have a higher upkeep factor (every footprint will be visible), they really lend a refined quality to the room.

HIDE AND SHEEPSKIN: These are great for small annexes in your room, or to fill an awkward space. I usually prefer to layer a hide over another rug for a luxurious look. I use a light-colored cowhide for a conversation nook that I have in my great room that didn't warrant another wool rug but really needed a floor covering. It provides a stylish but neutral accent for that area.

MANMADE: Want the wool look for less, or really want to change out your rug every few seasons? There are some really well-constructed synthetic rugs on the market. They are nowhere near as durable as your wool rug (some of which can last beyond 50 years) but they look good, and thanks to modern technology, they aren't terrible to clean either.

RUGS I LOVE

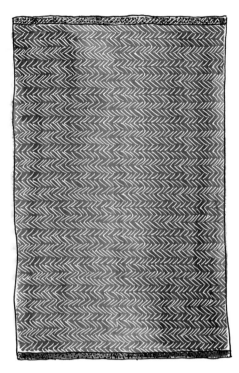

**HERRINGBONE HANDWOVEN RUG,
DASH & ALBERT**

This rug is inexpensive, durable, and has a neutral design that can complement many styles.

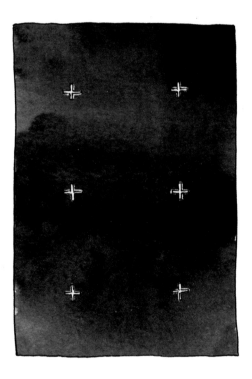

NORDIC KNOTS PLUS AREA RUG

This easygoing flatweave features a bold black design that is perfect for any modern living room. It lends an artistic touch to the living room without going overboard and overshadowing the room.

SAFAVIEH DREAM AREA RUG

I like this vintage-inspired look, with just a hint of color. It's versatile enough to go with multiple color schemes, but it's interesting enough to draw attention.

LIGHTING / SPLURGE

We went home recently for a family gathering, and my mom had redone one of her rooms, updating it with new tile and a modern look. Then we turned on the lights and . . . foul! She had installed a cheap overhead light that cast a blue fluorescent glow. Not pretty. Underinvesting in lighting, and not thinking about how to light your living room, can really get in the way of creating a room that feels welcoming and cohesive.

I'm not saying that you need to invest in a statement lighting piece in every room, but lighting is what sets the mood for your living room. You want to make sure it works for the space.

COLOR MATTERS

First, lighting color is important to think about. Definitely change some element of your lighting if it's too cool (i.e., too blue), too bright, or too fluorescent. If it's possible, a light bulb replacement in a warmer hue is an inexpensive way to create an updated look. At Havenly, we get really picky about the color of the lighting, for good reason. Too blue, and everything can feel too harsh; too yellow and you run the risk of things looking dingy (particularly in a bathroom). So consider a soft white to give a warm and comforting look to your room.

PRO TIP: The warmth of lighting is measured in something called Kelvin colors. I'm particularly partial to a 2700K or 3000K light bulb, which gives everything a soft white glow, without being too yellow.

MIX IT UP

The second key tip with lighting is what we call layering. Consider investing in more lighting if you don't have enough mixed lighting levels in the room. In other words, you should have light sources that emit light in multiple horizontal planes. So even if you have recessed overhead lights, think about a mix of table lamps and floor lamps to give you more control over the atmosphere of the room and a layered lighting look. The variation in light source is also helpful so you can change up the lighting for romantic dinner dates (on the sofa, watching *The Bachelorette*, obviously), or turn the brightness up for game night with the family (you need good lighting to catch your sister cheating at Scrabble).

Also consider the ceiling height and natural lighting in your living room when you put together your lighting scheme. If the room has lower ceilings, try to use uplighting to draw the eye upwards, and avoid heavy pendants or chandeliers that are likely to feel like they're reducing the ceiling height. Similarly, dark rooms benefit from recessed lighting to create an ambient glow.

Ideally in your living room (presuming it's not huge or tiny) you'll have:

· Three to five overhead or taller lights that are dimmable.

· Two to four table or floor lights. Consider adding one to two lights per 250 square feet.

ART / SPLURGE OR SAVE

As you choose art for your living room, it's worth it to think critically about what you have and what the room needs. This is not the place to let the room down; rather, art should be what elevates an okay living room into a sublime space. The art you choose should say something that's meaningful to you. I mean saying something in the figurative sense (please don't buy those "Keep calm and carry on" word art prints). We lay out some art tips below, but I realize that you, like everyone else, have art pieces that have sentimental value to you. So if you find yourself "breaking the rules" to keep those pieces, that's okay. You do you.

In general, toss or repurpose your art if:

IT'S A CLICHÉ. Have a framed poster of Van Gogh's *Starry Night*? (I did!) Monet's waterlilies? Unless you're the lucky owner of an original by the masters themselves, consider putting that mass-printed piece elsewhere. Cheap art prints of overexposed pieces look generic and don't bring much to the table.

IT'S WORD ART. No. Don't do it. Sometimes a framed quote done tastefully is gorgeous, but if it's on a wood block and it has something like "Live, Laugh, Love" on it, it's probably not interesting enough for you. You're interesting, darn it. Your walls should reflect that.

IT'S TOO SMALL FOR THE WALL IN YOUR ROOM. Too-small art pieces hung along a large hall will feel dinky, and will remove the power of the art. When Jason and I moved into our current home, I was coming from a historic house with a small living room. So I suddenly went from having little space for wall decor to having a sweeping open-style home with tall, vaulted ceilings. That meant that instead of the small-but-purposeful pieces that had adorned my living room walls, I now needed two large statement works to avoid having the space look awkward. Too-small pieces of art will make the space appear unfinished. If you do have some pieces that you love but that aren't size appropriate, consider filling out the walls around the pieces with a gallery wall of found objects or photography. This will not only create depth but will also complete the look on the wall and avoid the pieces looking awkward. You can also consider reframing a smaller piece of art with a larger frame with matting to create a more appropriately sized piece.

IT'S TOO MATCHY-MATCHY. Try to keep the art in a room varied. There's nothing wrong with a diptych or a matching set on one wall, or framing an architectural element, but if you have matching art on all the walls, the room won't have that finished and "designed" look. Split up your matching pieces, and find contrasting and interesting pieces to create interesting wall coverings for your living room. Art is one of the best ways to be playful with color palettes and styles, so don't be afraid to add a new pop of color to your room with your art selection, or mix modern art into a traditional room, and vice versa, to create more complexity.

Keep your art if:

IT'S SOMETHING WITH MEANING. Our director of design has an incredible portrait of her grandmother that hangs as a statement piece in her dining room. I love how it weaves in a little bit of her story, and also adds a vintage piece to her Brooklyn home.

IT CAN WORK COHESIVELY IN A GALLERY WALL. Tempting as it may be to just free-hang all of your small art pieces to haphazardly create a gallery wall, you're going to want to plan it out a little bit, to avoid the wall looking like a mess. Collect your items, use a level and painter's tape to plan things out, and buy or find items that are a mix of sizes and colors but that complement each other. (More on this in the Styling section.)

IT'S WHAT YOU LOVE. Your art is and should be a reflection of you and your tastes. Have fun with it. This is where you can really break the mold by adding art that has a different feel from the rest of the room, or add in playfulness in an otherwise seriously designed room. While you want the colors and style to play nicely with the remainder of the room, don't be afraid to be a little more bold in your art choices. I have a fairly classic and neutral living room, but I really love abstract art, so went with two big, bold pieces, with colors that are complementary to the room but bring a little bit of modernity to the space.

SOME OF MY FAVORITE (INEXPENSIVE) ART SOURCES:

Artfully Walls: Artfully Walls specializes in a large variety of framed art from interesting artists but at affordable prices. One of their Kate Roebuck pieces graced my living room for years, and I'm always impressed by their ability to have such a variety of artists and pieces printed at prices most of us can afford.

SaatchiArt: Not the most inexpensive option, but as far as editioned or collector art goes, SaatchiArt offers a relatively affordable assortment. You can buy a piece for as little as $200, which sounds like a lot for one art piece, but you can be sure that you'll have a truly unique work.

My own paintbrush (with the help of a good framer): In multiple places throughout my house, I've framed my own watercolors. If you are crafty, or have a little bit of an artistic streak, show it off. I typically buy large-scale watercolor paper and paints from Amazon, and on a warm day, I go outside and create away. I frame the best pieces through online custom framers (my favorite is Simply Framed, for large-scale art), and they look like professionally done art pieces. I tell myself that anyway. Regardless, it's a great way to showcase some of your (or your family's) art skills, inexpensively.

BEDROOM

What do you think of when you think of your bedroom? If we have done our job, the words we hope will come to your mind are *relaxing* or *peaceful*—not *unorganized* or *cluttered*. It's hard to feel serene and relaxed in a bedroom that isn't living up to its potential. There's nothing worse than feeling as if your sometimes-chaotic life is infringing on a space that's meant for relaxation and sleep.

When I lived in my previous home, I never felt like my bedroom was serene. Something about the color of the walls was too bright, the room was too cramped and cluttered, and I made the mistake of not investing in light-occluding blinds or shades in my southern-facing bedroom, so I always woke up with the rising sun. Frankly, the bedroom can sometimes be the last thing we think about when we design our homes. We tend to overthink our living areas, and by the time we are finished obsessing over every detail in the living room, we are too exhausted by the time we start to think about decorating the bedroom.

I eventually moved to a new home and realized that I had an opportunity to be more intentional about creating a beautiful bedroom. It was a very large space, but I wanted to be sure that it felt like a comfortable and cozy respite from my sometimes-frenetic life. I also wanted to use the extra space to create calming vignettes where I could lounge and read books, or hang out with a cup of tea.

I encourage you to not let your bedroom be the last room you think about. Aim for a room that is comfortable and peaceful, where you can recharge and relax. Clear out the clutter, add in a bench or chairs so you have places to sit (besides the bed), and ensure that you invest in comfortable bedding.

In general, I suggest a more uniform and restful color palette in the bedroom. The bedroom is not the space to go crazy with a cacophony of contrasting bold colors, but you can keep the eye moving around the room with different textures. That doesn't mean you can't be bold with darker walls or richer colors, but rather, try to minimize variation in color so that the theme doesn't feel too unruly or hectic. Most importantly, choose things you really love for this room, it will help you feel at home in the space that is dedicated to you and you alone.

BED / SPLURGE

Bigger is better here, as long as the bed you choose will fit your space without getting in the way of the flow of the room. Plan on making the bed in your main bedroom the largest that the room can tolerate; if you're upgrading in space, you'll want to consider upgrading in size if your budget allows. We upgraded to a king bed a year ago, and sleep (and life) has been so much better; my husband no longer complains that my tossing and turning wakes him up, and our dog has plenty of room to snuggle. Here's one point to keep in mind: you want to ensure that you have enough space around your bed to get in and out of it. So if you have a smaller bedroom, you may not want to choose a king-size bed. In a smaller bedroom, having a too-large bed ups the cramp factor. And no one wants to wake up and walk right into a wall!

Another point: a bed frame isn't optional! Please don't put your mattress on the floor and call it "modern." (Yes, we've seen people do this—and you know who you are.) Every bed needs some sort of elevation, but, more than that, nothing screams "frat boy who didn't grow up" more than a mattress on the floor. The headboard and bed can be minimal, or you can consider a platform if you like a more minimal profile, but I personally love a classic upholstered bed to add a level of lushness to a room that, I think, can handle it.

When redesigning a bedroom, we like to start with the bed choice. The bed is central to the design, and you can use your bed selection to think about how the elements in the room balance each other. You still have a choice here though: do you want your bed to be the centerpiece of your design, or a neutral complementary element to the rest of your room?

DIRECTIONS FOR YOUR BED

STATEMENT BED. Have this be the fun, larger-than-life piece in your bedroom. This could mean either a bed or headboard in a bold color, or a bed that has a bit more visual weight—for example, a modern canopy bed. Dramatic beds that I've loved in the past include those that have a large-scale tufted velvet headboard as well as my personal favorite—a modern four-poster bed. These beds create drama in the room and add a lot of immediate visual interest.

NEUTRAL BED. You can choose a versatile and less dramatic piece that will complement many different color schemes and styles. This approach likely has more longevity, and you can always play with the colors and textures of the decorative elements or bedding to create interest. Styles that are more neutral include a low-profile clean-lined bed, the minimalist-style platform beds, or even the tailored wingback styles in a neutral fabric. Ultimately, something that is versatile and not as trendy or large will offer you the most avenues to decorate.

Keep your bed if it fits the room and is sturdy, functional, and comfortable. But most importantly, keep it if it is a good bed, and mattress, that allows you to sleep well.

Get a new bed if you don't have a stylish and functional frame or if your mattress is uncomfortable. There's nothing worse than not getting a restful night of sleep. If it's a mattress problem, instead of buying a new bed and mattress, you can always get an inexpensive memory foam mattress topper from Amazon to up the comfort factor.

LINENS / SPLURGE

If you're doing a bedroom reboot, changing your linens is the easiest way to change the look of your room. And it's an element you can refresh without breaking the bank. I love spending a little extra on nicer bed linens because nothing feels better than slipping into crisp sheets at the end of the day. Definitely toss your linens if they're old and frayed, and consider new linens if you're still stuck with a nineties-style comforter with a dated paisley or floral cover that you can't remove and wash. You'll find high quality but affordable options for duvet covers and sheets with a lot of the newer online brands such as Brooklinen and Parachute.

Have you ever seen a beautifully styled bed and wondered why your blankets never look that cozy? We'll cover that in the Styling section, but for now, think about layers and texture. The ideal bed has a few layers to it, and you can use both texture and color (and mixing patterns and solids) to create the coziness that will ultimately lead to a "can't wait to get to bed" feeling to your bedroom.

When we redesign rooms, we almost always suggest new linens, as they really can be an inexpensive way to completely change the look of your bedroom. Just like decorative pillows and rugs, you can switch them out relatively inexpensively to get a big upgrade for not a lot of money.

When in doubt, don't dismiss classic crisp white linens. Suited to nearly every style imaginable, a basic white sheet set can be layered with interesting throws and pillows to create a scene that is elegant yet easy to maintain.

For my go-to sheets, I almost always choose a crisp cotton. Cotton is a natural fiber, which makes it more breathable (read "not hot!") and durable than synthetic fibers. This category has a lot of options, but details that will help you differentiate one selection from another include how soft the sheet feels and the level of luster and silkiness to the sheet. You've probably seen words like *percale* (a fine-textured flat cotton) and *sateen* (a silkier look), both of which refer to how the fabric is woven. There is also a lot of marketing around sheets that boast a high thread count, which is basically how many threads are fit into one square inch of the fabric. In laymen's terms, the more threads, the finer and softer the finish. However, I honestly think there is a lot of room for personal preference here. I prefer a heavier flat-finish sheet that feels crisp, while my mom likes a softer and lighter touch. Before you settle on anything, feel a few sheet sets to see what you like, and don't worry too much about the marketing.

Another lovely but less affordable option is bedding that is made of linen. Linen is a natural fabric, like cotton. It has become increasingly popular for sheet sets but has always been well liked as a material for duvet covers. Linen is a great solution if you find yourself getting too hot while sleeping, as it's

even more breathable than cotton. The look of linen is pretty specific, however; its slightly crinkly look and lack of sheen can lend a casual feeling to a space. If that look appeals to you and you're willing to spend a little extra, consider linen.

Other premium bedding options include flannel (great if you're living in a cold climate and want a cozier bed) and even silk (increasingly popular for pillowcases, since I hear that silk can offset premature wrinkling). All of these are excellent choices, but you won't go wrong with a simple cotton or linen sheet.

Some of my favorites:

Brooklinen Pure Luxe Core Sheet Set
I use this on my bed, in white. These sheets are smooth and crisp, and come out perfectly after a wash. The best part? They are sateen, which means they have a smooth and silky but still crisp feel.

Parachute Linen Sheet Set
If you're looking for a breathable and cool set for the summer, Parachute's linen sheet set is wonderful. They're durable (linen will last longer than cotton in most cases), and they come in a number of colorways—so you can enjoy the softness of this linen in any style.

NIGHTSTANDS AND DRESSERS / SAVE

NIGHTSTANDS

A key consideration in picking the right nightstands is the proportion of the nightstands to the bed. You don't want extremely delicate nightstands next to a heavily upholstered king-size bed. Similarly, you don't want nightstands that are too much taller than the height of your bed, which is measured as the top of your mattress.

We also think that while nightstands with open shelves look clean and simple, creating some hidden storage with a closed nightstand is a functional option to reducing clutter and keep your space feeling relaxed and serene. You'll likely need a covered area for personal items like medicine, books, and tissues, as there's nothing better than feeling like your necessary things are close by but out of view.

DRESSERS

While I'm usually all for a piece made with solid-wood construction, dressers are actually a place we usually recommend people save, if they're tight on funds. With the advent of MDF (Medium Density Fiberboard) and RTA (Ready to Assemble) products, you can often get plenty of storage at a really good price. The critical component of choosing a dresser is to make sure it works with your space. Think about door openings, and ensure that they don't get in the way of the dresser drawer openings. Or if you have limited wall space, opt for a chest or armoire that is taller than it is wide, to take advantage of vertical space.

Get rid of your dresser if:

THE STORAGE ISN'T ENOUGH. This is an item that you want to ensure suits your organizational needs. Make sure you have enough storage for your larger and bulkier items but also the smaller accessories (intimates, socks) in your dresser.

IT'S TOO MATCHY-MATCHY WITH YOUR NIGHTSTAND OR BED. You'll hear us saying this throughout the book, but nothing makes a design feel unsophisticated as having every item from the same store collection or finish. Choose shapes that are similar (say items that are both clean lined and low profile) but of different finishes (such as natural wood and white) to create a more eclectic but still cohesive look.

IT DOESN'T FIT THE SIZE AND SCALE OF THE ROOM. If a dresser is too big for the room, it can overwhelm it, and not in a good way. However, too small of a piece can feel haphazard or dinky.

OTHER BEDROOM STORAGE

Also consider buying an inexpensive place to put your phones, keys, and spare change. Using some sort of storage will help your room feel more organized, and it will keep the reminder of your day at bay in a space that is intended to be a reprieve from the chaos of daily life. If you have been obsessively watching and reading Marie Kondo, and admire her minimalist approach to things in your home, you can go a step further and just keep all of your daily clutter out of your bedroom to maintain a serene feel.

RUGS / SAVE

As noted in our tips on rugs in the living room, picking a rug for the bedroom has a lot to do with the scale of the room and the furniture. If your rug is too small for your new bed, you should toss it or find another place for it. Ideally, you have about 2 feet of the floor, on either side of the bed, covered with a rug. If you have a smaller room, or can't quite find the right size, consider putting smaller area rugs or sheepskin rugs on either side of the bed for a cozy place to put your feet in the morning.

For bedrooms, unlike living rooms, we'll mostly be okay with a "floating" rug, if that's what you have or can afford. (That's a rug that isn't fully covering the floor under the bed.) In particular, if you have a platform bed that lies directly on the floor, floating rugs are a nice option. However, the optimal situation is to have a larger rug, that extends on all three showing sides around the bed. It makes the room feel grounded and helps the rug feel substantial.

Consider using a softer rug—with a higher pile or more delicate materials, like silk. Your bedroom doesn't get as much traffic as your living room, so you can be a little less focused on durability here. Softer rugs feel better under your feet on those cold mornings when you have to wake up too early; they convey the feeling of cozy. I have a sheepskin in my bedroom, but I've also seen beautiful silk or flokati rugs used to great effect.

DRAPERIES / SPLURGE

Draperies in your bedroom are often more about function than in any other room of the house. You'll definitely need these to block out light for a good night's sleep, but from a design perspective, they can also add softness to the room. The problem is, draperies can be very expensive, particularly if you look for custom draperies, which are often necessary for nonstandard windows. I was shocked when we got our first quote from a custom drapery provider; it was much higher, by an order of magnitude, than I had anticipated. I ended up splurging on curtains for my main rooms, and to save costs, switching from custom drapes to premade ones in rooms that had standard-sized windows.

I couldn't be more happy that I splurged. Frankly, those French-pleated linen drapes in my bedroom make the room; they create coziness, block light, and just feel more finished.

Do not despair if your budget doesn't allow for custom drapes. If you are handy, or know a seamstress, you too can achieve perfect-fit drapes for less. We often suggest to our clients that they buy off-the-rack draperies, but to order ones that are on the longer side. (You can get very inexpensive ones from places like IKEA or J.C. Penney.) Measure them against your existing windows and go to a local tailor or seamstress to have them shortened. Just remember, you'll want to hang your drapes high and wide, so ensure that they are long enough to brush the floor when you hang your curtain rod as high as it will go. And, as a final step to make your drapes perfect for your bedroom, you can also buy blackout or thick lining fairly inexpensively at a fabric store to effectively limit excessive light.

Get rid of your draperies setup if:

THEY DON'T GET CLOSE TO THE FLOOR. You remember when you were a teenager and you realized your jeans from sophomore year were too short in senior year but you wore them anyway? Not a good look. Same with too-short drapes. Don't do it! As far as length, you have a couple of options.

My preferred option is having the drape just touch the floor, with a slight break. It's the most designed-looking solution. The key here is to measure and enlist a friend to help you hang them up so they're JUST right.

The drapes can almost touch the floor (less than a half inch above the floor). If you're not a fan of having curtains on the floor, or if you have little people or animals occupying the space and worry about dust and dirt, this may be a good option.

Another approach, if you like drama, or a more traditional, European-influenced look, is having the drapes long enough that they "pool" at the bottom. This is a great option if you're opting for a luxurious, substantial curtain (think sumptuous velvets) and you like a romantic, feminine vibe.

YOUR CURTAINS AREN'T HUNG HIGH OR WIDE. Okay, this shouldn't make you get rid of your drapes, but you should definitely adjust your hardware and ensure your drapes are long and wide enough to accommodate. To be clear, if your curtains themselves are too short, it is still not optimal to "correct" this by hanging your curtain rod too low, by which I mean, installing the rod right above the molding at the top of your window. If you have vertical height to play with, make sure you have the curtain hung high; it's how you create a room that feels elegant, and it also has the benefit of adding height to a smaller window. Similarly, if your rod isn't wide enough, you will have your curtains hanging in your window and blocking light, which is also not a good look.

THEY DON'T BLOCK ENOUGH LIGHT. There's not a lot worse, in a bedroom, than getting too much light when you don't want it. For your best sleep, you want to be able to control the light that enters, and draperies are key to accomplishing this—another instance in which you don't have to totally toss out your existing draperies, but you may want to consider augmenting your setup. You can add shades behind the curtains for a layered but light-filtering option. You can also sew in thicker linings, or even blackout linings, if you have curtains that aren't doing their job.

Some of my favorite sources:

IKEA, Target, and J.C. Penney all have inexpensive off-the-rack drapes that you can hang as is or tailor. Most often, they're under $50 per panel, which really cuts down on the out-of-pocket expense for draperies.

For a more expensive option, Pottery Barn has ready-made options that range from $60 to $150 per panel. There's a lot of versatility in their options, but they're made in solid fabrics, and their drapes are a good medium between a custom look and the budget varieties.

For my custom drapes, I went with The Shade Store. Frankly, if you're going to splurge, you may as well have the company come out, measure, make, and install. They also literally have infinite options in terms of fabric, drape style, borders, and mechanics (cordless, corded, automatic, etc.). They are a great option if you have custom-sized windows, or are less confident in your ability to measure and hang drapes.

DINING ROOM & BREAKFAST NOOK

Traditional homes often have both a formal dining room and a breakfast nook near the kitchen. However, as the tradition of dining around a formal table has become less of an everyday thing, we find that a lot of our clients are moving away from having a separate dining room in favor of more casual seating. The kitchen is rapidly becoming the center of the home, and in a lot of recent builds, are designed to be ever larger as more families want to convene and eat together there. That is something for you to consider along with the needs of your family: do you truly need a separate formal dining room, or would you rather create a multifunctional space where you can eat dinner every day and can still host the family for Thanksgiving.

If you have a dining room, I suggest getting a little more creative with the design. The separate dining room is where we see people bringing in an interesting wallpaper or hanging dramatic chandeliers and art. Particularly if you are lucky enough to have a separate formal dining area that is separated from the rest of your house, I love to bring the drama, and differentiate the space from other living areas. Doing so will make the special occasions that merit the use of your dining room feel much more inspired, and stand out from your every day living spaces.

For Emily and me, the dining room of our family home is a room that we remember fondly. Our mother's art deco-inspired lacquered dining set and the floor-to-ceiling art on the walls made the room feel like the most special part of our house. It was the center of our home whenever we entertained our extended family, so I have memories of long laughter-filled Thanksgiving meals where we'd eat both turkey and my mom's Indian cooking while catching up.

DINING TABLE / SPLURGE OR SAVE

I think the dining table can be a splurge, or a save, depending on your budget and how often you plan on using the table. An affordable option is to dress up a less expensive or a simple but elegant table with great table styling (which we cover in Part III Styling). However, we admit to loving solid-wood dining tables that convey more of an organic element—and we feel that they will stand the test of time. The designers we work with at Havenly love sourcing wood dining tables with a live-edge element or a slightly rustic feel, as we believe a table with character makes a room welcoming, helping create a place where you'd be excited to sit down for a meal.

Get rid of your existing dining table if it's too big or small for your space or feels unstable. Like so many other foundational elements in a room, if the table is too big, you or your dinner guests won't be able to get around properly. If it's too small, it'll make the room feel unfinished or lacking refinement.

Consider keeping or repurposing your dining table if it's of solid construction and fits the space. If you don't love the finish, consider a DIY refinishing job or having it repainted so it goes with your dining room aesthetic.

DINING CHAIRS / SAVE

This is where you'd want to save, as there are great deals online for dining chairs. However, when choosing dining chairs, consider carefully whether or not you want upholstered chairs. At Havenly, we see that so many of our clients love the look of upholstered dining chairs, but the reality of life is that things will spill when you're eating. In our household, I like to blame my kids, but in actuality, I like food with lots of sauces (and wine), and I spill just as much as they do. Having a chair you can wipe down is often helpful, but if you really want something more upholstered, try leather or vinyl-covered upholstered chairs. These materials can be easily cleaned in a pinch but they are also still comfortable to sit on. Sellers of modern-style furniture, like IKEA or even Design Within Reach, offer a lot of options that have clean lines, a more modern look, and a surface that's easily cleaned.

My personal favorite, for a classic style that combines easy maintenance and style, are bistro chairs that are in a rattan or woven plastic; they are easy to wipe down but provide a timeless look. (Check out the Riviera chair at Serena & Lily, but you can find more affordable options at Wayfair.) If you must have upholstered dining chairs, go with a performance fabric and look for options that have removable slipcovers. I use upholstered dining chairs with a linen slipcover in my formal dining room so when our four-year-old spills during Thanksgiving dinner (the very rare occasion that I let him eat on those chairs), I can spot clean them in the sink. If it's a really big mess, the slipcovers can be removed and dry cleaned (or in the worst case, replaced relatively inexpensively).

You do want to ensure that your dining room has some harmony between your chairs and table, but I like a more eclectic and interesting look, so we typically advise our clients to avoid choosing furniture from the exact same set. In order to mix and match dining chairs with your dining table, make sure to keep an eye on achieving harmonious proportion between the elements. Mixing a more classic dining table with Scandinavian or modern chairs can make the room feel a little less expected and certainly far more interesting than just buying a set from a furniture store.

Some of my favorites:

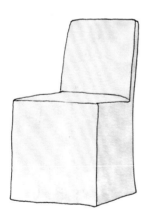

PARSONS SLIPCOVERED COLLECTION, RESTORATION HARDWARE
This collection has a lot of things I look for in an upholstered fabric dining chair—clean lines, a timeless aesthetic, and the slipcover makes for easy (read: kid friendly) cleaning.

RIVIERA SIDE CHAIR, SERENA & LILY
One of my favorite bistro chairs that come in a bunch of colors. I love the casual look of these chairs, and also the fact that they're easy to clean.

Okay, phew! I know that's a lot to go through, but I think that gaining a good understanding of what you have and what you'll need is key to getting started. It gives you a sense of where to focus and what to consider first. Now that you've worked through your entire home, hopefully you have a list of items that you may be in the market for. Now you need to figure out your budget and which, if any, of these items you'll upgrade, given your financial constraints.

SAMPLE BUDGET RANGES FOR AN AVERAGE LIVING ROOM

	BUDGET	MODERATE	SPENDY
Sofa	1000	2000	3500
Coffee Table	300	550	1000
Chair	300	700	1500
Rug (8'x10')	300	800	2000
Lamps (2)	120	400	1000
Throw Pillows (3)	90	165	300
Side Table	100	300	600
Art (3)	300	800	2000
Pouf/Stool/Add'l Seating	100	200	500
Decor Accessories	100	300	500
Window Coverings	100	400	800

COLOR ME PRETTY

Color is a critical matter for you to consider when you start to design your rooms. Color sets the mood for your home, and it can serve as a unifying thread for all the rooms in your home.

A lot of your color palette, like much of your designs in general, will be influenced by your everyday style, so it's worth thinking about what you're most drawn to in the world. Look at what you wear on a daily basis: are there colors you love the most? Keep in mind that your color palette can change with different rooms throughout your house, but it's often helpful to pick a theme and try to have that continue throughout your home.

From now until the end of the book, we'll be helping you narrow your options. After all, if you're anything like us, you want EVERYTHING! You see a pretty room and you think "Oh! Maybe I can do that in my guest bedroom." There's nothing wrong with having eclectic inspiration, but if you take it too far, eventually your house may look as if you had different people design each room, and then, if you're like us, you'll feel a little sad. Worse, then you have to go through the trouble of redecoration, which is a lot of work. By the way, if you end up needing to redecorate, or if you're not entirely happy with your results, do not despair. Sometimes it takes months, or even years, to collect the right items and find the right place for everything in order to create the vibe you envision for your space.

But I digress.

Let's start with some of the principles of color.

COLOR THEORY is the idea that different colors evoke different emotions. For example, warm colors are energizing and stimulating, while cool colors evoke serenity and calm.

To help understand color theory, take a look at the color wheel on the next page. You may have seen it somewhere between first and second grade and then forgotten all about it. Why are we dredging up memories of elementary school? As it turns out, the color wheel is a handy tool to start to plan out which colors you want in your space. It removes all of the "will this go, or won't this" guesswork from putting together your ideal color palette.

COLOR WHEEL

If you have a color you love for your space, but are having trouble identifying accent colors to create depth, look at the color wheel. How do you use the color wheel, you ask? Well, you can follow a few of the rules below.

ANALOGOUS OR ADJACENT COLORS are literally adjacent, or next to each other, on the color wheel. If you choose one dominant color, a great way to add depth is to fill in with adjacent colors. For example, if you decide to start with the color blue, adding greens or purples as accents to your color scheme can add interesting variation.

COMPLEMENTARY COLORS are across from each other on the color wheel. If you've fallen in love with one color scheme but want to add additional pops of color for variety, think about complementary and adjacent colors. This is a way to create a high-contrast and brightly colored palette for your room—but it is, often, a highly vibrant look, and not for the faint of heart.

MONOCHROMATIC color palettes are ones that include different shades of the same color. Using a monochromatic palette is a simple and accessible way to get started with your design.

I like to follow the classic 60-30-10 design rule for incorporating colors. Pick a color that you love to be the dominant color in your room, and then weave in a little bit of other colors to create contrast and interest. The ratio should be something like 60 percent in your dominant color, 30 percent of the secondary color, and then a sparingly used accent color in 10 percent of the room. Use the color wheel and color theory to pick two to four additional accent colors. Love blue and want to use it as the dominant color in your office? Think about persimmon (complementary) or green (adjacent) as accent colors. Or just go with different shades and textures of blue for a monochromatic look.

To get started with your color scheme, I like to suggest that you start with inspiration, so let's walk through a few color schemes and show you how some of our clients applied them to their spaces. If one inspires you, think about how it may work in the reality of your room. Do you have warmer-toned wood floors? How would that look with a cooler color palette? If you fall in love with a brightly colored modern look, think about how that might work if you have a more traditional home. But don't stop with the photos in this book—go to art fairs or vintage furniture stores and see if there are pieces or elements that you just love, and use those pieces to inform the color scheme in your home.

NEUTRALS

A neutral color scheme is like the little black dress of design. It's very chic right now, and it does seem to go with all types of styles and architecture. Despite this seemingly tame color palette, using neutrals is actually a very exciting way to decorate your room. How do you keep the room from looking completely boring? The key is to think about using other elements in the space to create a pulled-together look. You can add pops of color, play up textures, and think about metallic elements to finish off a neutral space.

If you're dreaming about a serene bedroom or are drawn to a zen-feeling living room, go with neutrals. Neutrals will help your space feel calm, collected, and organic. The best part is that neutrals are incredibly versatile; you can use them in a variety of ways, but we most often use them to convey a relaxing and airy feeling.

One way to get started with a neutral color scheme is to identify your perfect "white" base, because a perfect white wall color goes a long way. But white comes in so many different shades that you actually must contemplate what kind of white you like.

If you are lusting after serene and clean white walls, consider the light in your room in order to select the perfect white paint. If the room you are considering gets cool light (perhaps you have a north-facing room in a cool climate), consider warming it up with a paint color that is more creamy, instead of a pure cool white. If you get a lot of lovely south-facing light (lucky you!), go with something crisper for balance. I used Benjamin Moore Chantilly Lace throughout my house, which is a cooler white with blue-gray undertones, because my house gets a lot of warm Denver sunlight. However, in my basement and in some of the bedrooms that don't get as much light or are northern facing, I went with Benjamin Moore's White Dove. This particular white has a creaminess to it that helps avoid a dingy blue tint in rooms with less light.

FAVORITE WHITE PAINTS

Benjamin Moore Super White: This white is a true white, with absolutely limited undertones. Think of it as the brightest and purest white there is. Good for a more modern and incredibly crisp look.

Benjamin Moore White Dove: There's a creamy quality to White Dove, which makes it remarkably able to warm up a space, and it pairs really well with warm wood floors. Because it doesn't feel stark, it's great for spaces with less light.

Farrow & Ball Ammonite: This is another softer color that is great when you want to warm up a space. This one has a slightly grayer undertone than White Dove, which pairs beautifully with natural woods and organic elements.

Benjamin Moore Chantilly Lace: A bright white with a slightly cooler (or bluer) undertone, this one is perfect for a crisp look, and because of its lack of an inherent tint, it goes well with so many other colors. Also great for trim.

Once you've selected your white base, start to layer on other tones and textures. A really well-done neutral room looks breathtaking, not boring, and so varying your shades is very important. Don't go all beige, trust us, that doesn't always end well, and you'll end up with a room that vaguely reminds you of tapioca pudding (yuck). Instead, bring in different tones of color—creams, whites, and beiges—to create subtle variation for the eye and bring a sumptuous feel to the room.

If you're decorating with neutrals, remember, textures are your friend. Really amp up the different materials and textures to create visual interest in place of colors. Think about a chunky knit throw, or a textured flokati or shag rug, and mix tones of wood to bring warmth and layers to your neutral living room.

Finally, with neutrals, consider small touches of pattern or color. I sometimes like to bring in hints of dark colors, like black, in hardware or other details to ground the space, and provide a little contrast and depth to an otherwise lightly colored room. You can also bring in some patterns to keep your eye moving around the room, and if they are used effectively will really make the room feel like a "designer did it." You want the room to feel purposeful, like you personally chose each individual element to work in harmony together, not like you did a color filter search on Wayfair and just bought everything that was "taupe."

Which leads us to . . .

BLACK AND WHITE

Does anything go better together than black and white? This color combination can be bold or subtle and offers a lot of versatility across all rooms and styles. The best part? It never goes out of style (unlike the unfortunate orange wall-to-wall carpeting in my childhood bedroom in the 1980s).

Black is also the grounding component of nearly every color palette. It can add dimensionality to a pastel room, avoiding the "I'm just out of second grade" feel in more whimsical palettes. It can also bring much-needed interest to a room that's clad in neutrals.

There are a couple ways you can go with this color scheme. You can create something bold and high contrast, lending an air of drama and glam to a space. Alternatively, you can use black as an accent to offset the lightness of the room, which will create a more subtle look. Either way, choosing a black and white color palette is a very sophisticated style statement in interior design, just as it is in fashion.

PALETTE 1

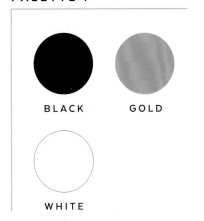

BLACK   GOLD

WHITE

PALETTE 2

BLACK   CREAM

GRAY   WHITE

PALETTE 3

LINEN   BLACK

CREAM   GOLD

MUTED CLASSICS

This is the most traditional feeling of all of our color palettes. From a sunny yellow to a muted green, the color scheme is all about bringing in color as a neutral. If you go this route, make sure you break up the colors across your rooms by using crisp white trim (although I've seen some interesting trim combinations recently, like a lighter wall with a blue-gray trim), and try to keep all of your rooms in similar or adjacent color families. (Don't do a burgundy red dining room next to a deep navy living room.)

In the living room featured opposite, the pillows are green and traditional blue, and while there are black accents, the gray, blue, and green theme is repeated throughout the home. Cohesion is the critical component to avoiding looking too, shall we say, unsettled?

That being said, don't be too matchy with your colors. For example, if you like navy blue, don't just use that shade of navy blue as your only color accent throughout the room. Weave in other tones of blue, a leather or wood grounding element, and a few layered neutrals to create a more intentional and adult feeling. If the eye only sees one accent color, it tends to get both bored and overwhelmed at the same time. And that isn't good, people.

PALETTE 1

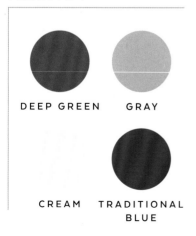

DEEP GREEN   GRAY

CREAM   TRADITIONAL BLUE

PALETTE 2

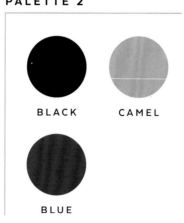

BLACK   CAMEL

BLUE

PALETTE 3

BLUE GRAY   WHITE

COGNAC   CREAM

PASTELS AND SOFTER COLORS

Soft and feminine, pastels are having a moment. Whether it's a blush pink throw or a muted mint green lamp, the new pastels feel totally fresh and can dress up an otherwise blah room. Since this is a bit more of a trend, you can ease your way into this palette without feeling as if you'll need to spend lots of money to redecorate when it goes out of style, by pulling the color in through decorative accents. Accessories like throw pillows are more easily replaced than, say, sofas. That way, you can indulge in something that feels fresh and unique, while feeling confident that you won't be stuck in a dated room when the trend passes.

Use pastels if you're looking for a neutral look but want to play with color and are looking for a softer, almost romantic, feel. We're seeing some beautiful rooms with accents of pale blue and sage green. I'm also loving blush, particularly when it is paired with creams, camels, terra cotta, and neutral wood tones to add a little gravity.

In the bedroom opposite, our designer Amy mixed in light blue and blush tones, but the room doesn't feel overwhelmingly pastel due to the grown-up neutrals and gray patterned wallpaper in the room. (This is good: you don't want an adult bedroom to feel like a nursery.)

PALETTE 1

CREAM   CAMEL

BLUSH

PALETTE 2

MINT GREEN   CREAM

BLUSH   COGNAC

PALETTE 3

PALE BLUE   CAMEL

CREAM

BOLD OR PRIMARY COLORS

Bold colors can really spice up a room. How do you get away with it without it overpowering the room and anyone who sits in it?

We want to make sure we get the most important point across about color: avoid matchy-matchy color schemes. Do we sound like a broken record yet? In other words, don't just pick one shade of turquoise and repeat it (and only it) throughout the room. The key is layering in other colors and shades. If you like bold colors, pick your primary color and layer on different shades of that color, alongside other bright accent hues in the same theme, to create a cohesive and variable look. Don't be afraid to use contrasting colors! This is the color scheme that can really bring personality into your space.

You can also break up color overload by using neutrals effectively. Use brown leather accent furniture next to bold accent chairs, or neutral walls as a backdrop to brightly colored pillows to avoid the risk of overstimulation. When colors are done correctly, a person entering a brightly colored room shouldn't notice the colors themselves, but rather, feel like they're walking into a composed but cheery space. So pick the individual elements you want to feel dramatic and bright, and avoid having every item in the room be high contrast and bold. Then make sure every bright element has a neutral anchor point to ground the saturated color.

PALETTE 1

MELON   BLUE

GREEN   GRAY

PALETTE 2

BLUE   PINK

LEMON   CREAM
YELLOW

PALETTE 3

GREEN   CREAM

CAMEL   BLUE

MOODY HUES

I love this color scheme for rooms that have lower light to begin with (think basements or windowless powder rooms). And why not lean into the mood? This palette brings the drama and really can take your style to the next level.

In the living room opposite, our client used navy, a very bold wall color, to accent her lighter furniture and colorful pillows. The black doesn't feel overly gothic, or even dark, it just serves as a punctuating factor for her moody living room. It's sophisticated, and conveys drama without being over the top.

PALETTE 1

HALE NAVY   CREAM

CAMEL

PALETTE 2

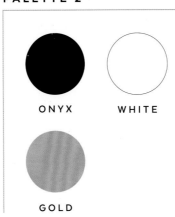

ONYX   WHITE

GOLD

PALETTE 3

DARK GREEN   GRAY

CREAM   COGNAC

JEWEL TONES

The jewel-toned palette incorporates rich, saturated colors like emerald green, fuchsia, and royal blue. To pull off a jewel-toned look, similar to our considerations with other bolder color combinations we've discussed, we like to start by choosing a base color, preferably a neutral, and then incorporate adjacent or complementary tones. You definitely want to limit the different types of colors you choose here (when in doubt, use the rule of three, page 204) to avoid looking too busy. Any color scheme that incorporates a lot of brighter colors will feel like a riskier look, but as a result, if done well, you create a space that is truly unique. What I love about jewel tones is that when the colors are paired with rich fabrics and are offset by crisp neutrals, the combination works to create a luxurious feel. I've seen jewel tones work especially well in statement dining rooms or formal living rooms, areas where you can imagine wanting to bring a luxe feeling to a space.

PALETTE 1

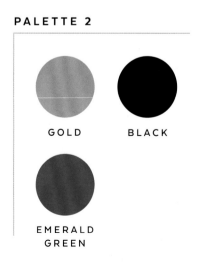

NAVY   BLACK

ROYAL BLUE

PALETTE 2

GOLD   BLACK

EMERALD
GREEN

PALETTE 3

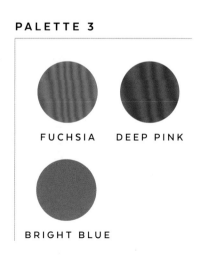

FUCHSIA   DEEP PINK

BRIGHT BLUE

MAKING DECISIONS
ABOUT COLORS

With all of these beautiful palettes, and millions of color combinations between them, how in the world do you choose? We think there's a simple question that may help guide your decisions:

How do you want your room to feel?

A   Dramatic

B   Light and Airy

C   Calming and Cozy

D   Playful and Whimsical

If you choose **A** (dramatic), try moody colors but don't rule out black and white, which, due to the high-contrast factor, can really bring the drama. I recognize that it can sometimes be hard to carry the moody color scheme through an entire home—it can feel exhausting or too dark—so we recommend choosing selected spots in which you will go with a darker wall and moodier palette. We often see dramatic looks in a study or dining room that is adjacent to a room that has lightly colored walls, but uses moody accents pulled through in the textiles or pillows.

If you choose **B** (light and airy) or **C** (calming and cozy), consider light neutrals or pastels, and bring in lush textures to create a cozy or calming feeling. For people who chose light and airy, we've also seen blue and green accents be popular, in particular if you like your space to have a beachy or coastal vibe.

For **D** (playful and whimsical), consider black and white or bright primary colors. Don't be afraid to mix complementary colors (for a reminder, check out our color wheel graphic on page 81) to get a fun vibe. We love a more playful color palette; when edited well and anchored appropriately, it can really bring personality to a room. If you aren't quite sure about bright colors throughout the home, consider bringing in more color and whimsy in select areas. We see a lot of kids' rooms, and even powder rooms, that are a little more bold in their use of color, bringing a sense of play into your home without oversaturation.

One thing to also think about when you choose your colors is how risky you want to be in your space. Do you want to change your design often and continue to incorporate the latest trends, or would you prefer to have a more classic style that stands the test of time? If your tolerance for color risk is high and you're open to a more dramatic color palette—have fun with it! This is the opportunity to let your personality shine in your home. Love bold colors but want to mitigate some of the risk? Instead of investing in brightly colored furniture items, bring in the color via art, throw pillows, and rugs, all accent items that are easier to replace.

When we started working with Blair, she was living in a Brooklyn loft but was finally ready to move into her recently renovated 1925 bungalow in Florida. Since Blair is a fashion influencer known for her love of colors, patterns, and dramatic shades, we knew we'd have a lot of fun working with her. After an 18-month renovation, she was ready to add her own personal touches to the space but was having trouble mixing the classic style of her home with her love of colors. She wanted personality but also sophistication—in her words, she didn't want the house to feel too "obviously Florida" (think flamingo motifs and palm prints).

Blair knew she wanted a bright, vibrant design, mixed with modern elements, so we brought in lots of colors and patterns in the art, rugs, and pillows along side neutral elements, like the marble coffee table and leather sofa. We kept the walls fresh and white, to better showcase her energetic art collection and create a look that was daring but not too "on the nose."

Notice, in the space shown on the opposite page, how we used color theory to create cohesion, even though she used a lot of colors in this playful space. We used some complementary colors (the blue and pinks/oranges), as well as adjacent colors, to great effect—to create a space with a ton of personality.

When I decorated my house, I knew I wanted to keep a few rooms relatively neutral. I live a hectic life and travel a lot, so I wanted my home to feel like my sanctuary, and I wanted to fulfill my vision through a calming color palette. I was lucky to move into a house with multiple living areas, but for my formal living room, I really wanted a look that was elegant and airy but also timeless. I felt I could invest more in pieces for this room if I knew the style was likely to last for a long time.

This room plays on variations of creams and whites with some blue accents. We brought in comfort with a cream rug with lots of interesting texture, and then contrasted that with coffee tables in a neutral blue range and white chairs with nailhead detail, to create some variety in the space while still retaining that feeling of serenity.

We used decorative elements, like black accents on the coffee-table books, or the lushness of the greenery, to bring in contrast and ground the light and airy space. I have grand visions of how I can continue to add texture and variation in this space (design is never done!), but you can see from these photos how this living room won't go out of style anytime soon. The cream-and-blue-plus-texture combo is a true classic.

PLANNING YOUR SPACE

EVERYTHING
IN MODERATION

Have you ever walked into a room and felt it was too crowded, making the space feel cluttered and stifled? Or a space that felt as if it was too empty, lending it an unfinished air? The tough part of decorating with furniture is the dimensionality; it's hard to understand how things may look in your space before you actually put it all in place. Honestly, even the best designers make mistakes here. This stuff is hard! However, thinking through how the elements in your room work together is what we think makes the biggest difference in creating a well-composed and well-designed room.

Here are some terms to know for this discussion:

Scale and **proportion** refer to how pieces fit together and how those same pieces fit a space. This is the most mathematical part of design, but your eye can immediately identify when something feels off. Scale refers to how well your pieces fit in your space. Proportion refers to how well your pieces fit together in terms of size.

FLOOR PLANNING

Let's work through some things to consider as you think about planning out your space. You'll want to get a sense of the basic orientation and placement of the key elements of your room, and also identify which foundational items you'll actually have room for.

Here's what you'll need to get started:

- a measuring tape
- a friend or partner
- a notebook

Spend some time thinking strategically about your space. First, identify what you're going to be using the room for. Do you need a lot of space for your kids to play? Is this a formal room that won't get used a lot? You'll use this to decide how much articulation room you need. If the room doesn't get a lot of traffic flow, or you like intimate seating arrangements to allow for conversation, you can arrange the furniture a little bit tighter. If you have toddlers constantly running around, make sure there's enough room in between things to avoid unintended bumps and bruises.

Next, identify features of the room that you can't move. You won't want to block doors, windows, fireplaces, etc.—so make sure you leave some clearance around each of the features and try to work each one into the design. The best-designed rooms are thoughtful about architectural elements, so if you have a full-width picture window with scenic views, consider making that a focal point of your room.

Then, also consider whether your room has a natural focal point. In some rooms, the furniture layout is obvious; for example, in most living rooms with a fireplace, the main seating area faces the fireplace, as it is traditionally the focus of attention in the room. In other rooms, a relatively square guest bedroom, for example, the layout is a little more flexible. In these cases, you may want to try different orientations to see what feels most natural to you and most functional, given the purpose of the room.

Finally, measure your room and draw a floor plan. Use a friend to help you get accurate measurements, and check your math. So often I measure a room and then I realize that in my diagram that opposing walls are different sizes, when they should be the same size, for example. Once you have the floor plan, start thinking about your room in blocks. Draw in a block for each of the foundational elements that you intend to have in your room. In larger rooms, you'll also want to think about subdividing the space for different activities. For example, in an open-concept kitchen and great room, you may have blocks for your breakfast nook table and blocks for your sofa, chairs, rug, and coffee table. As you start to place things conceptually, remember to think about clearance around furniture (you'll want 3 to 4 feet for a walkway, and generally 30 to 36 inches of clearance around your items).

PRO TIP: An iPhone can actually measure a wall. We think the Measure app is super easy. (Just make sure you double check the accuracy by measuring the same wall a few times through the app.)

As you draw these blocks, you can and should play with different orientations, if the room allows for it. The easiest way to accomplish that is to consider the biggest space taker in the room and imagine how you might switch the placement of that object. Can you move the sofa to be away from the wall? Can you rotate the bed to a different wall? In my home, the obvious placement of my sofa may have been against the wall on the left of my great room, but I realized that by rotating the sofa, and "floating it," by which I mean moving it slightly away from the wall to give it breathing room. I could create a delineated seating area in my open-concept space.

But wouldn't it be nice to actually feel what it's like to walk around in your space? In the old days, we'd even recommend taping cutouts on the floor and walking around your room to simulate the flow of your space. Nowadays, we at Havenly rely on creating 3D models to virtually simulate, photorealistically,

what your space may look like when everything is in it. Basically, these steps give you a feel for whether things feel too close together in the room, given what you're planning to buy, or whether the room feels too empty and spare. Different people have different tastes around spacing, so doing a walk-through, either virtually or in real life, gives you the opportunity to consider your family needs too. For instance, now that I have small children, I'm more sensitive to clearances because the kids will knock things over if they're too close together. (Thank you, clumsy toddler phase!) You'll want to consider space and clearances for adults, too. I'm under 5 foot, 2 inches tall, but what might the clearances feel like if you're very tall? What feels comfortable for some people may not be enough space for others.

PROPORTIONALITY AND THE RULES

Proportion is the difference between a room that feels composed and a room that feels as if it were designed in a piecemeal way. A few years ago, I had an inherited sofa that I had lugged with me from New York City to Denver. It was brown leather, and while a little traditional for my tastes, it was serviceable, and I felt it could be used again in my new home. To spruce it up and fill my new large living room, I bought a coffee table off the Internet, in a reclaimed wood finish. When the table arrived, I unpacked it with a lot of anticipation, but when I stepped back to assess the look of the room, the table looked very out of place. The finish was lovely, and it felt like a substantial piece of furniture, but my sofa had been optimized to fit the living room in my small Manhattan apartment, and by comparison the coffee table was a very large piece of furniture. The sofa and table just didn't go together: the width of the table was too broad and the height was too low relative to the seating elements. Adding the coffee table had the effect of making the living room feel like what it was: a mash-up of different furniture bought at different times instead of the adult and sophisticated space that I had been hoping for.

The most important guideline when considering proportion is to ensure that all of your items have similar heights and scales. For example, the sofa seat and back height should each be within a few inches of the seat and back heights, respectively, of any accent chairs in the room. Similarly, the height of the coffee table should be no lower than 1 to 3 inches from the height of the sofa seat. Try to optimize for horizontal levels, so that multiple pieces are on the same plane; that will ensure that you have a few different levels in the room to achieve a look that feels really put-together but not too one-note.

#1 RULE OF THUMB: THE GOLDEN RATIO

There are no hard and fast rules in interior design (in my mind, rules are meant to be challenged!). However, the golden ratio is a good rule of thumb to help you achieve balance in any room. If you have an interest in math, you've probably heard of the golden ratio, and you may have even heard why human beings find this ratio so pleasing, but that's for another book. To simplify, just think about a rule of two-thirds or one-third as you think about planning out your space.

What does this mean? Here are some examples:

> When you think about how large your rug or furniture should be, think about covering about two-thirds of the floor.

> When you think about the size and scale of wall art, think about having the art you hang cover a third of the open wall space.

> When you're styling a coffee table, think of the maximum height of objects as being a third of the height of the table.

> When you are thinking about two adjacent pieces of furniture, like a coffee table and a sofa, think of having the coffee table be nearly two-thirds of the size of the sofa.

In other words, if you use this very easy rule of thumb to find pleasing proportions for all of your pieces, it'll help ensure that you're achieving a well-balanced room.

#2 RULE OF THUMB: SYMMETRY AND ASYMMETRY

Balancing symmetry and asymmetry is another key to creating a visually pleasing room. You'll want some items that are symmetrical (or paired on each side of the room), and in other areas, you'll want to create asymmetry, which calls for mixing elements that aren't necessarily matching.

Think of symmetry as a mirror image. In particular, rooms such as the bedroom or dining room, or rooms that have large architectural elements, typically lend themselves to more symmetry—where each side of the room is reflected in the other side of the room.

Asymmetry is often used in larger and more versatile rooms, like living rooms or kitchens, where you have a variety of seating or other items. Getting asymmetry right requires a common thread throughout all the elements, whether it's a style or color and pattern, so that it still feels pleasing and cohesive.

How do you know you've gone too far? If you're looking around your room, and everything is in matching sets and pairs, you may have too much symmetry. This can actually make your room look a little unrefined (or #basic). You can mix things up by adding different pillows, adding a new color, or moving around your furniture to create more exciting combinations.

Similarly, if your room feels chaotic, cluttered, and messy, you may have taken asymmetry too far. Think about adding in some matching elements or ensuring that your decorative elements have a common theme.

Emily's glam living room in NYC, shown above, provides a great example of symmetry balanced with asymmetry. I love that the room is definitely symmetrical yet no one side of the room feels too much like a mirror image of another. It's harmonious without feeling chaotic, which is achieved by the similar-scale furniture. Also, would you not die for those backless chairs?

As we think about planning your space, let's walk you through a few items and considerations to ensure that your space feels well balanced and designed.

Roughly 2/3 the length of the wall

SOFA SCALING

Because the sofa is typically the most dominant element of your living room, getting the scale right is tremendously important. Think about using the two-thirds rule to determine which sofa would work best for you. How do you apply it here? Well, for one, you don't want the sofa to be the full length of the wall (or room) that it's being placed against. You also don't want a sofa that feels too small in proportion to the living room. Think about finding a sofa that's sized to be roughly two-thirds of the length of the side of the room on which you'll be placing it. Similarly, if you're buying a sectional, ensure that each side also leaves enough space to avoid it feeling too oversized.

However, your preferences can come in here, as well. Sofas are typically standard sized, 72 inches, 84 inches or 96 inches. If you measure your wall and it's 140 inches long, two-thirds of that is 92 inches. You can either go with the 96-inch, if you'd like more seating and have the sofa take up more of the room, or the 84-inch, if you'd prefer to keep it a little bit smaller. You may also factor in the depth of the sofa: a 96-inch width with a 40-inch depth will likely feel pretty large in the space, depending on the remaining dimensions of the room, whereas one that has a slimmer profile will feel more petite.

LIGHTING SIZING AND PROPORTION

If you're going for statement lighting, you obviously want to make sure that it looks right for your space. But how do you make sure it is not overwhelming for the room or too small to create the impact you're looking for?

It's simple! If your lighting fixture is over a dining table or kitchen island, break out the two-thirds rule again. You need to find a chandelier that is about one-half or two-thirds the width of the table. Have you fallen in love with something smaller, or do you just want more lighting? Feel free to double up lighting fixtures to create additional drama.

A dining room fixture's diameter should be ½-⅔ the width of the table.

32-36"

32-36"

7' above floor

Hang your chandelier about 3 feet above the dining table (or kitchen island) for good lines of sight when you're sitting down at the table—while still allowing for the chandelier to feel present and important in the room. And if a room has extra-high ceilings, consider a two- or three-tier chandelier to create even more drama.

If your lighting fixture is a focal point of any other space, you can also use a little bit of math. Add up the length and width of your room in feet, and use that as a guideline for the diameter or width of the lighting fixture in inches. In other words, for a room that is roughly 10 x 10 feet, you'd want a lighting fixture that was roughly 20 inches.

You can use the rule of one-third to figure out how tall the lighting fixture should be, and where you should hang it. You'd want the bottom of the fixture to be a little less than one-third of the distance between the ceiling and the floor where it is hung, but at least 7 feet above the floor, to allow for proper clearance.

DRAPERY SIZING AND PLACEMENT

"High and wide" is the rule for drapes in all rooms of your home. "High" doesn't mean that you have to hang your hardware all the way at the ceiling, but if you have plenty of vertical height between the top of your window trim and the ceiling, it will look odd if you hang your curtains just an inch above your window. Hanging them wide means leaving plenty of room on either side of the window for the drapes to gather. Hanging drapes this way can visually create the illusion of a larger window.

As far as the drapes themselves, we address this in the first chapter, but make sure they're both long and wide enough for your window. From a length perspective, please do not install draperies that do not at least nearly brush the floor (leave those half-length drapes for your aunt Edna's house). To keep the drape from feeling too insubstantial relative to your window, you're also going to want to ensure that each panel is wide enough to cover the window. Consider going for a double-width drape for a wider window.

As an example, in the image of a dining room on pages 130–131, you can see that there's a lot of symmetry, as is often the case for dining rooms. We made it feel harmonious by sticking to a clean coastal theme, but added in organic elements with greenery and the substantial dining table. Our design goal was to make the room interesting while keeping it from feeling too predictable.

SMALL SPACES

I want to explore a broader trend that we are seeing, specifically among our younger or urban-dwelling customers. More and more of our clients are forgoing the larger homes in the suburbs in favor of living closer to urban centers. As a result, we have a number of clients asking for our help in making a small space—everything from tiny homes to studio apartments—feel livable. Small spaces, when the design is done right, can really come to life and even benefit from their cozy feel.

When it comes to proportionality for small living spaces, ensure that the size of your furnishings fits the small scale of the space. (Are you noticing a theme here? This chapter is all about that cohesion.) Your space will feel bigger when it's not crowded with too-large items. Also consider the silhouette of your items: a piece that has raised legs or a more delicate profile will feel lighter than a piece that sits directly on the floor.

A few key considerations when designing small spaces:

MAXIMIZE STORAGE. If creating built-ins is out of your budget, explore modular furniture solutions that can be customized for your space to give the look of custom wall-to-wall storage. When you have a place for everything, it'll cut down on the clutter and create the appearance of more space.

EDITING IS YOUR FRIEND. With smaller areas, you have the obligation to actually get rid of the furniture and accessories that you don't absolutely love, because you don't need to fill extra space. What is it that Coco Chanel said? "Look at yourself in the mirror and remove one accessory." Get rid of (or store for a future home) the extra dresser or side table you don't love anymore. Replace it with more storage, or some greenery, to create the feeling of more space.

BUILD VERTICALLY. Consider installing shelves on the wall instead of buying a bookcase, to free up precious floor space. In many well-designed small spaces, clients maximize their vertical area by adding shelving and storage all the way to the ceiling, to add storage, but still keep plenty of floor space even with limited square footage.

CREATE LIGHTNESS WITH SILHOUETTES AND FABRICS. Replace heavier-feeling items such as velvet draperies or high-pile carpets with lower-profile items, like linen curtains or flatweave rugs, to help create airiness that will also keep the eye moving.

BRING THE LIGHT IN. Bring more light into the space by adding layers of light and ensuring that every corner has a soft white light source. Play up the windows by placing a framed mirror opposite the window, which will immediately bring in more light and create the appearance of a well-lit space that will feel much larger.

One set of clients—a busy California family—needed to make the most of their informal entry and sitting room in their Los Angeles home. We suggested adding functional storage to the room that would stash away all sorts of knickknacks and beach gear but also create comfortable seating for their growing family. The result of the project is shown above. I have to say I love the unified and beachy color theme, which expresses a California cool vibe, but the mixed use of storage and seating mixes comfort and function, reduces clutter, and provides a casual area for the family to enjoy time together.

For Vivian, above, her 700-square-foot condo in Denver needed to mix both style and practicality. She didn't want her smaller space to cramp her style, and so she installed a built-in desk and bookcases that allowed her to showcase her eclectic collection of books and photos without making the space feel cluttered. What I love about what Vivian did is she broke a living room convention to great effect. She felt that she didn't need a traditional sofa but instead wanted seating areas that allowed for her and her husband to relax together at the end of a long day. Indeed, in the space she had, if she used a sofa, she would have risked not having enough space for sufficient seating. Instead of a sofa, she chose a pair of matching chaises to face the fireplace, which maximized the seating area while bringing an openness to the narrower living room.

PART II

THE STYLE
BREAKDOWN

YOUR STYLE DIRECTION

We've gone through a lot of interior design basics in the previous chapters. Hopefully you now feel as if you have the foundation on which to start to decorate your dream home. So far you should have:

1. A list of things to keep and toss

2. A budget

3. A sense of colors you love

4. A perspective on the right layout for your room

5. A list of things you need to buy

The next (and in our opinion, most fun) step is figuring out your style direction. We are biased, because we own a design company, but we think you should do this before you buy a single new piece of furniture. After all, there's nothing worse than buying something that ultimately doesn't fit in with your vision.

In my last house, for example, I was super excited about buying a Herman Miller rocking chair. I loved it . . . until I realized that I really wanted my home to have a more traditional vibe mixed with glam, and the chair looked super out of place in the context of that style direction. I was sad to give it away. But ultimately that's what I did because no matter which room I put that chair in, it felt awkward. It just didn't belong. And much like a good relationship, you can't force a style fit.

Take it from us: thinking through what speaks to you for your home will save you time and money later. That's the surest way to land on something that will feel right both now and down the line. The alternative—finishing the project and not being satisfied—is no fun. It's a big letdown to spend money and then feel like you did it all wrong.

We know there is no one-size-fits-all approach to styling one's home, as each space is as unique and distinct as the person who lives in it. Even so, think of the following pages as a go-to primer in which you can explore different styles. We like to think about this section as a set of style recipes: we'll set you up with some guidance on what main items to start with as a foundation, and then you can add whichever spice and seasoning (or in this case, accessories and furniture!) to sprinkle in to make it your own.

When we work with clients, the first step to choosing a style direction is to get them to verbalize what they want. We often find that this step is incredibly daunting for most of our clients, as so many of us aren't familiar with design phrases or aren't used to connecting our own likes with a specific style itself (or aren't as confident saying what our likes and dislikes are, for fear of sounding inexperienced). We've seen so many people become more confident in themselves and their design decisions when we arm them with the information and terminology to speak about their specific tastes and design style. Folks often become bolder when they know they belong to a specific "style." We often make an analogy to selecting wine. I spent time in the tasting room of a vineyard ten years ago, and so many of the customers had pretty strong likes and dislikes, but they found it hard, and sometimes even embarrassing, to articulate exactly what those preferences were. It was only in tasting a number of wines and hearing the staff put words and terms to what they were tasting that customers started to have confidence in talking about their preferences and making wine selections.

That's why we always encourage our clients to take some time to browse inspirational images in order to get to know themselves and their own styles before embarking on the design process. That way, there are no surprises down the line, and you have a solid framework from which to work. (For example, in theory you think that you like brown leather sofas, but when you see a picture, you realize that's not actually your style. Conversely, you may be inspired by a weathered antique dresser when you see what it looks like in the room, although you would have never chosen that piece on its own.) Context is also key: showing the overall look and feel of rooms helps guide clients into figuring out what mood and feel they are trying to evoke in their space. By going through the style recipes in the Finding Your Style section, you will emerge better informed and more comfortable with what your likes and dislikes are, which will eventually lead to solidifying your tastes before moving through the design journey.

Having a strong style direction to start with will help make the whole process move more quickly. When you're working from a consolidated style perspective, you'll be a master of editing your choices and your existing items. You won't be tempted by pieces that don't fit within your style vision, and you won't waste money on items that don't belong within your overall look. A lot of our clients ask us about varying their styles across different rooms in their homes, and we typically say that you can have fun and be playful, but to create cohesion, we advise you to think about variations within your dominant style family to have your home feel collected and harmonious.

That being said, I've never seen a room that I love that strictly adheres to one design style. The best rooms have strong foundational elements in consistent styles but are able to bring in elements of others to create interest and a sense of personality. Don't be afraid to mix global elements with a more modern style—or add an unexpected antique touch to a contemporary look. Layering different stylistic elements breaks you out from a cookie-cutter room to one that feels, well, uniquely YOU. After all, you don't want to come home to a living room that looks exactly like the generic one in the West Elm showroom, do you? No one wants to be #basic.

FINDING YOUR STYLE

HOW DO YOU CHOOSE
YOUR STYLE?

Take a look at what you're drawn to in other areas of your life.
I always suggest thinking about what you really love to wear,
but you also could consider hotels, restaurants, or other homes
that you love. What elements do you admire in a space that you
covet? What makes you feel most beautiful when you consider
putting on a killer outfit? Keep a notebook and try to identify the
stylistic elements that pull you in. Do you like the oversized drum
shade on a chandelier in a hotel lobby? Maybe the contrasting
patterns on the chairs in your best friend's house catch your
attention. Start training your eye to find the things you like and
the things you don't.

Some of the things we most commonly hear people say they want
in a space include:

Gold or brass accents

Natural elements, like reclaimed wood and linen textures

Greenery

Furniture that is lighter in color

Cozy throws

Neutral colors

White or lighter walls

Blacks or blues as an accent color

What we commonly hear that people do not love:

Literal or generic art

Purple

Over the top ornate items

Overly traditional silhouettes (rolled armed sofas, heavy fringe)

Once you've identified some of your likes and dislikes, start to home in on where you fall on the style spectrum of modern or traditional:

- Do you love rooms that feel edited and minimal, with less clutter, geometric shapes, and clean lines?

- Do you prefer the warmth of a room with a maximalist feel, complete with delicate elements and furniture with fine details?

If you chose the first, you're probably leaning toward a modern style. If you chose the second, consider styles that are more classic.

The truth is styles aren't easily categorized on a strictly linear spectrum and we think many style categories have a lot of overlap. Look at the images in this section and see if particular images or words jump out at you. Are you looking for something urban and on trend? Or are you on the hunt for something a little more effortless and casual?

CLASSIC STYLES

Let's talk about the classic style—a style that evokes glamour and elegance by making use of symmetry and visual balance. If you're an Old World Bordeaux-loving bookworm whose idea of color is wearing cream and who happens to despise chaos, this is the style for you. This style often suggests serenity, calmness, and peace while also creating a space of friendly comfort where every item has a specific place. This style is influenced by traditional European decor, which makes it timeless, elegant, and so sumptuous.

In classically styled rooms, fabrics with traditional patterns, such as nature-inspired prints, plaids, or stripes, adorn upholstered armchairs and sofas, while mirrors and art are hung symmetrically around focal points in the room. If you have any antiques or hand-me-downs from your grandparents, this is the style that best lends itself to their use. This style is often characterized by neutrals, but when color is used, you may find rich warm tones accented by dark wood finishes.

HOW TO SELECT YOUR ITEMS

Rules of design aren't that complicated, and you'll find us repeating a lot of the same principles throughout this book: scale and proportion, color, texture, and editing. But as you get started with the classic style, try to pick a color theme for your space. Typically, more traditional styles have muted color palettes—either lots of neutrals or rich, deep colors.

Once you've chosen the colors that speak to you, move to the big items in your room, or your foundational pieces. In a more traditional look, these will be the most design-forward pieces in your room, and they will help set a timeless and classic tone. One of the principles that is often used in this style that evokes elegance is symmetry. Classic styles really double down on this, using it to balance out patterns and textures. Furniture is usually grouped in settings that facilitate conversations, and pieces are arranged around the natural focal point of the room. What this means in practice is living rooms that have symmetrical seating arrangements anchored by a sofa, and dining spaces that all match up perfectly. That said, your pieces don't have to be total mirror images of each other, on either side of a room, but rather the room itself should feel balanced. A classic living room arrangement will involve you placing two chairs opposite your sofa and layering in matching lamps and art on opposite sides of your room, so that your space really feels composed and symmetrical.

When choosing furniture, try to find pieces with softer styling—rounded elements, tufted details, delicate trim. If you're looking to go full-on classic, try to avoid sleek angularity and harsh lines, which can clash with a more traditional look. Incorporate upholstered pieces—with subtle patterns—to give your space a little bit more depth. Use tailored skirts, whether on your bed or your sofa, to exude an upscale and old-fashioned feel.

TIPS TO ACHIEVE THE TRADITIONAL OR CLASSIC STYLE

USE TEXTURES! Traditional and classic looks often have a more muted color base but mix in different fabrics and materials to create a layered and interesting look. Consider mixing luxe materials—like velvets and silks—into your traditional look to create some formality, but prevent it from looking too stuffy by adding in some pieces in cleaner silhouettes and modern and casual fabrics. (Think about adding items that have traditional lines but are upholstered in twill or linen, or adding in a side table with clean lines next to traditional accent chairs.)

MAKE GOOD USE OF FEMININE DETAILS AND CURVED LINES.
Consider an oversized chandelier with curved arms, or tufted details and turned legs on your furniture. Classic rooms often have items that feature decorative details, such as nailhead trim or ornate moldings around framed art, to add richness to the look. Think about the Queen Anne chair, with its curved lines and ornate legs, as a piece that embodies the quintessential traditional piece.

ADD IN MODERNITY, WITHIN REASON. The key to layering classic styles into a modern home is to add in elements that are a little cleaner and less fussy. Pair an antique armoire with an upholstered bed with simple lines, or a more traditional tufted sofa with eclectic pillows to make the look feel less formal. Mixing a little bit of contemporary with a traditional look keeps it looking fresh and avoids the "I walked into a Victorian era men's club" feel.

The bedroom on page 152 combines modern and classic styles, but you can see the classic elements in the upholstered bed and the nailhead trim around the ornate legs of the bench. I love the art deco-inspired nightstands next to clean-lined table lamps and simple art. With these motifs, this bedroom will truly stand the test of time (unlike, say, my nineties bangs).

DOING THINGS ON A BUDGET

We know that oftentimes budgets are tight, and there's a lot of stuff to spend on when you're moving or redecorating. We can't always afford editioned art and investment furniture. Here are some tips on getting the items you like while still having a happy bank account:

1. Look for deals at flea markets or on Craigslist. These sources can be the most risky, but they also give you the best bang for your buck. Sometimes it's easy to repair a beautiful but broken item or reupholster a chair—and it's fun to make the piece your own in the process, too!

2. Think about buying investment-quality foundational pieces (sofas, beds, etc.) that you know you'll be able to live with for a while. That way, you'll avoid having to replace the items sooner than you'd like. The key is to recognize what is likely to hold up, particularly in a piece that gets a lot of use, like a sofa. Look for sofas with kiln-dried hardwood frames that are held together with nails. (You can test for this by holding the frame of the sofa and wiggling it a little. The piece that will last will feel sturdy with not a lot of wobble to the frame.) With upholstered items, know that a denser foam lasts longer but is less plush, so look for a mix of feather and foam if you like a plush sofa.

3. If you have great foundational pieces, you can save money by finding or making inexpensive decorative accessories. Think about repurposing throws into pillows, using Etsy to find custom draperies, or even painting your own art.

4. Know sales timing. We collect some data on this at Havenly to try and predict discounts, so we know that our clients who time purchases around days where you'll see large discounts—Memorial Day, Labor Day, and Black Friday—can save big. January and July are also great months to buy, as retailers are often clearing their shelves around these times prior to bringing in new assortments.

5. Look online, with Wayfair and Amazon. If you know what you want, you can find some smoking deals. Particularly if you're looking for an item where quality isn't a concern, and you're okay with ready-to-assemble furniture, these can be great resources to buy good-looking items at really accessible prices.

RELATIVES OF
CLASSIC STYLE

Currently, two of the most popular classic-related styles are what we call the modern farmhouse and California casual styles. These styles layer classic warmth with elements of modern simplicity. Often we're finding that these design styles, in execution, draw from Scandinavian inspiration, as well. Combining easy living and a timeless feel, modern casual and farmhouse styles are really having a moment. (Blame Jo and Chip?)

MODERN FARMHOUSE

This color palette is intended to be muted and clean, really playing up neutrals. Since you'll be using white in a lot of places, it's worth finding the right shade of white paint for your walls and finding complementary pieces to create more visual interest. (See page 88 for our favorite white paints.) Use your stylized and accessory elements to add in texture, and use colors to add in variation, so your room doesn't feel too bland.

NEUTRAL   TAN   BLACK   WHITE

MODERN FARMHOUSE
— ROOM RECIPE —

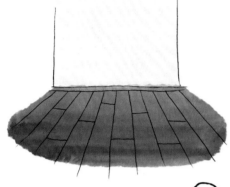

1 Start with a clean palette of wide-planked floors and light-colored walls.

2 Mix with classic elements like a traditional chair or painted shiplap.

3 Add in a dash of natural elements like a jute rug or a reclaimed wood table.

4 Accent with wrought iron details and black trim to create definition.

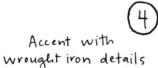

One of our Havenly design team members, Kylee, bought a new house with her husband because she was expecting twins and needed more room for their growing family. She really wanted a comfortable place to gather with her husband and kids and wanted a stylish but functional home. She was lucky to have a new-build home that started with the perfect white oak wide-planked flooring, and she really leaned into that design feature as she considered adding to her dining area.

The base palette for the room, which you can see opposite, is very simple: Kylee used a lot of white, mixed with the natural feel of the chandeliers and the linen end chairs. To bring a hint of color and warmth to the room, she incorporated decorative elements in black to add dimension to her light-and-bright dining area. I love the rug she chose; it adds pattern to an otherwise simple space, and the plaid really accentuates the modern farmhouse vibe. The modern lines of the striped draperies and pendants accent the more traditional styling of the dining table, and are balanced with the simplicity of the black farmhouse dining chairs.

This space combines traditional elements (the table, the rug) with a clean and modern setting to make it feel thoroughly contemporary. There's nothing stuffy about this dining room; it feels livable and not too precious. It feels like a room that Kylee and family can actually eat in every day without it feeling cluttered or unharmonious.

CALIFORNIA CASUAL
OR MODERN CASUAL

This is probably my favorite style, and when I moved into my new home, I used a lot of California casual influences throughout. Picture a breezy home in Santa Barbara where you can throw open your windows and kick off your shoes. California casual homes are decidedly cool—they feel relaxed but composed and almost always have an effortless quality. This style is reminiscent of the impossibly cool girl you knew in college, the one who always looked impeccably dressed in a crisp white shirt, with clear and glowing skin, even without makeup.

This style incorporates artisanal and found items, including the perfect wood cutting board, handthrown pottery, plaster vases, and warm rustic elements such as woods and natural fabrics. You should feel like the collection of items work together in an effortless way. To perfectly achieve this look, the key is to not try too hard and to let it feel a little lived-in. Like every other style, however, remember not to go overboard with too much accessorizing; find a theme for your decor pieces, stick with it, and edit, edit, edit. This look is intended to feel curated, not cluttered.

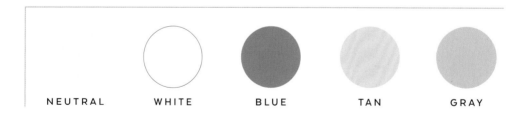

NEUTRAL   WHITE   BLUE   TAN   GRAY

CALIFORNIA CASUAL
— ROOM RECIPE —

1

Start with a clean palette of wide-planked floors and light-colored walls.

2

Add in found items — the key to a casual look is letting it feel effortless, instead of the more "finished" aesthetic of a modern farmhouse. Try some collected art, or some handcrafted throws.

3

Layer in different textures. Consider starting with woven materials and then adding natural or nubby textures.

4

Accent with hints of metallics with patina. Think aged brass fixtures with rubbed bronze.

THIS IS HOME

DREAM DESIGN LIVE

A mix of neutrals and contrasting colors creates stylistic interest while maintaining that easy-breezy look of a California casual space. Think a tumble of pillows in neutrals, mixed with some worn leather and linen elements, as a good representation of this style.

My formal living room, opposite, features a lot of elements of the modern farmhouse style. The textured tone-on-tone rug and the muted pillows and throws, combined with the linen drapery, lend it a more relaxed air. I wanted it to feel formal enough for entertaining but also comfortable enough for us to sit and read a book while sipping a glass of wine.

You can see that we added a lot of texture, despite the minimal use of color. The rug in particular adds a dimensional texture. I love how we used a little bit of greenery (including the olive tree that I stole from one of our designers) and the coffee-table books to create an organic look in an otherwise symmetrical (read "formal") space.

One of the trickier challenges in this living room was the height of the ceiling. Two-story living rooms are hard to design because they can sometimes feel cavernous and they don't exactly give you the warm vibes that we are looking for when it comes to California casual style. We broke up the white walls and helped disguise a nineties-style arch window that I couldn't change, by adding long custom draperies for some softness that also made the space feel more finished.

This room is where I go when I want to feel at peace. I do a lot of work here (including the writing of this chapter), and I love the slightly undone but still composed feeling that I get when I'm sitting here.

KYLEE'S LIVING ROOM

It may not be surprising that Kylee and I share a style. She executed a casual look in her living room with richer colors—and we're in love with the resulting space. She took a clean base and added sumptuous green upholstered chairs, black hardware and finishes, and warm woods and leathers to add a sophistication and dimension to an otherwise airy home. You can see that the casual style she implemented in her living room weaves in the connection to her modern farmhouse dining room that we featured on page 158. The styles are similar, and can be mixed and matched in a home for a cozy but elegant outcome.

PITY ABOUT THE TV

Remember the days of the big, bulky, ugly TV? When we had to build entire media cabinets to hide a TV in the living room? There are a lot of reasons to thank the universe for the invention of flat-screen TVs, but our designers are mostly grateful that now TVs can sit in the room, almost like a work of art, without bulky media cabinets taking up floor space. There have been some aesthetically pleasing innovations as well. Some TVs, like the Frame TV from Samsung, can turn the face of your TV into an art piece, so that the screen actually becomes a more intentional decorative element in the room.

Some people think it's taboo or unseemly to position the TV as the main focal point of the living room. I think there aren't rules around this, and you should optimize for what works for your family in that space. If you anticipate settling down to binge-watch Netflix in your living room nightly, and that's a large part of how you relax in your room, then orient your furniture around the TV. That's totally okay, and, in many cases, it's what's expected.

The one thing we caution you to think about is how to hide the messiness that usually comes with the electrical cords, HDMI cables, and other things that attach to the television. It's one matter to have a flat screen mounted on the wall, but no one wants to see cords snaking down the wall to electric and cable boxes, etc. This is one place where it's worth splurging a little: drop the cords through the drywall so you can hide them behind the walls, and invest in a streamlined media console to hide the Apple TV/cable box/Nintendo Wii (if you, like me, are a parent to video game lovers).

PARISIAN MODERN

Excluding pizza, there's nothing we love better than a look that combines heirloom pieces with the sleeker lines of foundational items that reflect the way we live today. We are obsessed with how a traditional element looks next to the clean lines that are found in contemporary furniture. There's a "je ne sais quoi" to this style, a mix of the modern with the glamour and drama of architectural details and ornate details. We also love Paris. So basically, this look is a win-win.

We think this style works best if the architectural bones of your space have a little bit of character. Did you move into a prewar apartment on the Upper West Side of Manhattan? Don't want to fully redo your nineteenth-century farmhouse? Lean into the history of your space by combining the ornate with the streamlined to create a layered, interesting look that is so perfectly chic.

PARISIAN MODERN
— ROOM RECIPE —

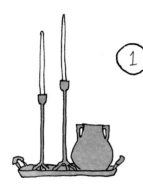

1 Start with your favorite antique items or head to a flea market to find pieces that really speak to you.

2

Add white walls and a generous rug.

3 Layer in ornate frames for your art, add dramatic moldings, and pile on lots and lots of books.

4

Add in streamlined modern elements that complement your classic pieces — think about a sofa with modern arms or a neutral coffee table.

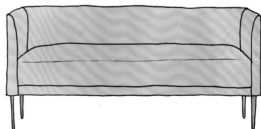

5

Hang a dramatic chandelier.

6

Revel in your Parisian modern space by enjoying a deliciously flaky croissant and sipping some café au lait.

SHELBY'S LIVING ROOM

We were sad when Shelby, our first designer at Havenly and our longtime head of design and creative, moved from Denver to Brooklyn when her husband, Chris, got an exciting job in NYC. We weren't alone. While she was excited to move back to NYC, she wasn't thrilled about leaving her amazing living situation in Denver. She had just bought and renovated her Denver rowhouse to completely suit her needs, and the idea of moving back to a rental apartment was not exactly appealing.

Leave it to Shelby to really embrace the bones of the Brooklyn walk-up that they found, as you can see in the photo opposite. I love the wood parquet floors and the medallions on the ceilings, which, combined with the plaster moldings, make the perfect base for a Parisian modern-style home. She plays into the theme by adding ornate frames to set off her eclectic collection of art, piles of coffee-table books, and traditional-inspired chairs upholstered in a modern fabric. The space still feels fresh, though, thanks to the dome chandelier, the contrasting clean lines of her sofa and chairs, and the bright airy space.

If you live in a rental, and have things that you can't hide (like an old-fashioned steam radiator, as seen opposite), consider using it as part of the design. By layering art and books on top of the nonfunctioning vent, Shelby works it into the design of her living room—almost as a structural piece of art—while maintaining its functionality.

COASTAL

I first spent time in the little town of Chilmark in Martha's Vineyard during my second year of graduate school. The home we were staying in was the epitome of coastal style, and my visits to those coastal New England homes inspired me to incorporate elements of coastal style into my homes on many occasions.

Coastal styles are meant to evoke life on a beach, but the best of coastal-inspired rooms aren't too literal. My favorite coastal rooms are breezy, beachy, open, and light. The best way to think about this aesthetic is to picture soft fabrics, neutral tones mixed with blues and soft greens, and textural components, mixed with a lot of openness and the use of natural textiles. Think seagrass or jute rugs, open floor plans, soft white draperies, and classic art. Natural wood elements are often light, and can be either whitewashed or stained in a light natural (preferably matte) finish, but you can also include rustic wood details.

Start with a neutral base of colors—something like a white, cream, light blue, or gray—and mix in a color that brings in that beachy feeling. Often coastal rooms mix in different blue tones, but don't be afraid to add in some warmer colors, such as deep browns or oranges, to create depth.

As is true of so many of the styles on the classic ends of the spectrum, the colors don't shout in a coastal room. Rather, the neutrals give off a relaxed and mellow feel, which sets the tone for the entire space. That said, usage of colors is encouraged. Complementary neutrals are always a good choice, but if you want to go beyond the usual blues and whites, try muted versions of your favorite color—a lilac, palm green, or even a soft yellow to add something a little unexpected. The trick here is to balance any brighter colors with surrounding accessories that are in softer tones and limit the brightest or most saturated colors to the decorative accessories such as lamps, pillows, and drapes.

COASTAL
— ROOM RECIPE —

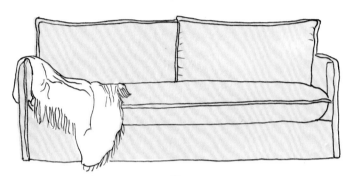

① Start with a base of crisp whites.

② Layer in pieces with natural woods, channel driftwood.

③ Shake things up with some accent pieces, preferably in shades of blue.

④ Ground everything with a natural jute rug.

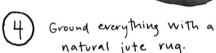

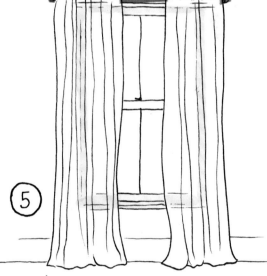

⑤ Add in breezy sheer draperies.

Put on your boat shoes and enjoy a cocktail in your beachy abode. ⑥

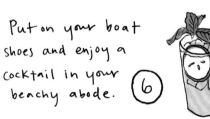

LUXE AND GLAM

Do you want to bring *alllll* the drama to your space? Do you love sumptuous fabrics, jewel tones, and glam details with accents of gold? Our modern glam lovers are the maximalists of interior style. Glam or Hollywood Regency style is inspired by the glamorous decor found in the homes of stars during the Golden Era of Hollywood. Luxe interiors lean heavily on luxurious accents and grand open floor plans. The goal is to really bring the glamour. If you love this style, you'll want to choose blingy accessories, lacquered surfaces, and simple shapes to fill out your space.

The client whose room is featured on pages 180–181 moved into her Connecticut home and wanted to up the glam factor of the house. We love her dramatic and fiercely bold dining room. The leopard-print rug, the Hollywood Regency chandelier, and the dark walls add to a completely creative but not too over-the-top room.

LUXE & GLAM
— ROOM RECIPE —

(1) Start with sumptuous materials, like velvets and satins, for your accent furniture. Consider adding a chair in luxurious jewel-tone velvet.

(2) Layer in touchable textures, like faux fur throws and area rugs.

(3) Add in glistening details in your favorite metallic or mirrored finishes. In particular, consider statement chandeliers and mirrored dressers.

(4) Think about lacquered paint, acrylic, and marble to finish out your space for your coffee tables and table lamps.

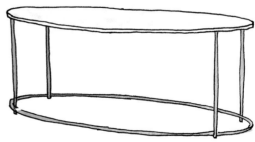

MODERN

Contrary to some beliefs, in our opinion, modern designs aren't the exact opposite of classic designs. It's also not true that you have to stick with one end of this spectrum. In fact, it's the combination of modern and classic styles that often yields the most chic and contemporary look. But what is "modern," anyway? Let's dive into the principles behind modern design a little bit, so that we have an understanding of how to incorporate modern elements into our homes.

At its core, the modern style was inspired by minimalism embodied in décor and furnishings typical of the 1930s. It has evolved to foster many different style trends, including mid-century-inspired designs as well as the ever-popular Scandinavian look. Contrary to some beliefs, modern design doesn't have to feel cold. In fact, by using colors and layered textiles appropriately, modern designs can feel organic and warm—while still maintaining the minimal look that is characteristic of this style.

To accessorize modern styles, remember to be itentional about editing. Nothing is attractive about a home that feels unintentionally bare. So, find items that create personality, but use them in moderation. Use plants or botanicals to bring in some greenery, or add to a statement gallery wall of found items to up the charm factor. Try to avoid accessories that are heavily adorned, and try and avoid too much stuff, in general; it's not modern to be cluttered. To play up the modern style's focus on clean lines and geometry, consider contrasting colors for your trim or accessories with a geometric feel to them.

Modernity, however, is so often about leaving room for personal interpretation and expression. One of my favorite parts of the modern style is that it so often involves making a bold statement, whether through an unexpected choice of colors or a unique furniture piece. There is nothing more modern than a design element that is a little controversial to drive conversation.

MODERN
— ROOM RECIPE —

Start with a base of neutrals
white, gray, or navy
are always good choices.

(1)

(2)

Add in a hint of color,
either something muted or an
unexpectedly bright element.

(3) Look for furnishings
with clean lines,
unfussy detailing,
and sleek surfaces.

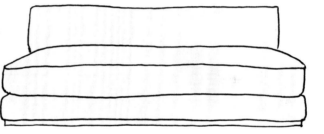

(4)

Mix in some geometric patterns or
sculptural decor elements.

It's modern to be bold and daring,
so use an unexpected art piece or an
oversized sculptural coffee table to
create an interesting focal point
(and a topic of conversation for your
bound-to-be impressed guests).

(5)

AMY'S LIVING ROOM

Amy had just had her first baby, and she wanted a home that was modern but still felt like a comfortable nest for her growing family. As you can see opposite, she incorporated some elements of color into a gray-white-and-black color palette and added surprising elements with art choices to keep the design interesting. She started with a modern-feeling-dark gray sofa and layered in geometric patterns with her throw and ottoman. She kept the look organic by adding an eclectic gallery wall and brought playfulness into the space with unexpected art pieces and a creative mini teepee for her pup, Biggie Smalls.

Because of the size of the space, Amy stayed away from a bulky coffee table, and instead made good use of a pouf in a geometric pattern, and a smaller side table. By utilizing clever storage, Amy's living room feels bright and modern.

MID-CENTURY MODERN

The term *mid-century modern* encompasses design trends that originated in the 1950s and 1960s. Although it remains popular even today, the style, which was ubiquitous earlier this decade, has started to evolve into a mixture of modern style trends. In the 1950s, this design style originated alongside a broader modernist movement in the mid-century era and led to the development of iconic pieces that you may recognize, usually designed by people like Eames or Saarinen. Even if those names don't ring a bell, you've probably seen the Eames chair in design magazines, as it regained massive popularity in the 2010s; tulip tables and womb chairs are some other pieces that are emblematic of this design style. Did you love every room you saw on *Mad Men*? Love color palettes that feature warm caramels and burnt oranges offset by walnut woods and leathers? This may be the style for you.

Mid-century modern as it manifests itself in design today involves many of the same natural materials, clean lines, and structural elements of other modern styles. We love this trend as it is easy to pull together and incredibly versatile. What's more, with so many of us moving to urban areas, it is quite compatible with smaller living spaces.

MID-CENTURY MODERN
─ ROOM RECIPE ─

(1) Start with a neutral base.
(We love a good white wall.)

(2) Add in muted primary colors
like blues, reds, and oranges.

Find items inspired by mid-century modern
designers with geometric legs and clean lines.
(Pick out your favorite Eames-inspired chair
from Amazon, for example.)

(3)

(4) Look for lighting that
has a sculptural feel
to it.

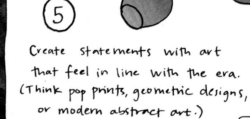

(5) Create statements with art
that feel in line with the era.
(Think pop prints, geometric designs,
or modern abstract art.)

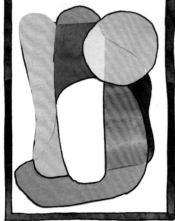

(6) Pour yourself
a martini in your
Don Draper-approved home.

CHARLES'S BROOKLYN APARTMENT

Another one of our clients, Charles, was in a transitional period in his life and wanted a space that felt done but had a lot of function for his young daughters. From the picture opposite, you can see that he incorporated classic mid-century shapes and items, but kept the room from feeling too expected with pops of color and interesting patterns.

We used a navy rug with a sophisticated pattern as a base, as we knew the darker color would stand up well to little feet but also ground the room. The rug's pattern incorporates mid-century elements, and it helps set off the clean lines of the other pieces in the room. The geometric legs on the coffee table and chairs all work in conjunction with the directly mid-century-influenced walnut media cabinet to create a cohesive look for Charles and his family. I love this apartment because it's not too literal but references mid-century style.

BOHEMIAN

Bohemian style is the most maximalist of modern styles. A mix of modern and traditional, bohemian style is usually composed of an eclectic combination of globally inspired items and modern accent pieces. A bohemian room feels rich and relaxed; it evokes artistic feelings by layering multicultural pieces with a simple base. The style is all about individuality. It attracts artists, free spirits, and world travelers alike, making bohemian style all about breaking the rules of design.

To create a modern bohemian style, start with a neutral base color. For instance, a warm white base would work well here, as would earth tones such as terracotta, green or rust colors. Allowing for a clean and consistent base ensures that the room doesn't feel too chaotic. Speaking of avoiding chaos, editing is still important in this style, if not even more so than with other styles. Bohemian rooms can risk feeling too cluttered.

Pattern and texture are the cornerstones of bohemian style—the more interesting, the better. Look for patterns that are rich and globally inspired, mixed with elements that look as if they've lived a life of their own. I love finding heirloom items in people's homes, to mix with vintage rugs and antique pieces. You want your bohemian-inspired room to tell a story of global travels and reflect your own personality.

On pages 192–193 you get a feel for the layered look of a modern bohemian style. By mixing the traditional side table with the streamlined leather chair, you get an artful mix of the old and new. Add in bright art and global inspired textiles, and you have a unique, free-spirited space.

BOHEMIAN
— ROOM RECIPE —

(1) Start by finding textiles that you love. Perhaps it's a rug or bedspread that speaks to you, preferably with interesting patterns and rich colors.

(2) Add in complementary accessories that draw thematic elements from the textiles you've found, either in pattern or color, to create an eclectic but unified look.

(3) Find low-slung furniture with clean lines to offset the explosion of patterns and color.

(5) Add bohemian elements with abandon: tassels, lanterns, poufs, and pillows.

(4) Head to an antiques store to find interesting items that really speak to you, or find those packed-away mementos from your travels.

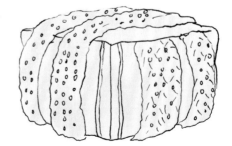

MARRYING YOUR PARTNER'S STYLE

Does this scenario sound familiar? You love your wife. She's wonderful, kind, smart, funny, and does the crossword with you in bed on Sundays. You wonder how you got so lucky. But somehow, when you moved in with her, you just couldn't agree on what to keep, toss, and buy, and the ensuing conversation veered toward potential argument zone. Her minimal modern style just didn't vibe with your love of all things rustic.

This happened with me and my husband. I would characterize myself as borderline tacky-glam. Remember when every member of the Kardashian clan had an identical home with a black-and-white checkered foyer and brass-and-mirrored accents galore? Yeah, that's me. My husband, well, not so much.

This may be one of the most common questions and design dilemmas we get. The reality is, marriage and interior design mix really well, as long as both parties are willing to see the beauty in each partner's style. I actually think that combining styles is the best way for a uniquely personal living room that really works for both of you. As they always say, marriage is a compromise, and mixing your design styles is a part of that compromise you committed to!

I guess the way I'd say it is, like in all potential conflicts of opinion in relationships, you both have to identify what is and what isn't important to you, and communicate what your needs are, what your nice-to-haves are, and what your absolute non-starters are with each other before venturing down the designing journey together.

Some of the most successful spaces we've designed have combined a more modern or industrial aesthetic with classic accents. For example, we love seeing a more traditional desk paired with a modern Eames chair. I've also enjoyed spaces where we added interesting dimension to a very light and airy space with a leather bench or natural wood accents. The pairing of different textures in that scenario works really well.

Here's what we typically suggest: talk about each room and what you want the overall feeling of it to be. The reality is, in order to have a design that feels cohesive, you'll need to choose an overall design style for that room and add in complementary accent pieces that reference other styles. So let's say your husband loves the clean lines that come with modern design, but you opt for a more feminine and classic look. One option is to go with a more modern look for the basics of the room (think the big pieces—the bedframe, the nightstands, the dresser), and then add in ornate or classic elements around the foundational pieces. For example, you can choose a more modern sofa and a coffee table with cleaner lines, but then layer in a pair of accent chairs with some glam and flirty details, or an ornate gilded mirror above a mid-century modern console. You can also layer a modern space with chandeliers and lighting that is more classic to create a unique and thoughtful look.

SOME OTHER QUICK TIPS TO MARRY YOUR STYLES (PUN INTENDED)

SHOP TOGETHER. Make sure you have an "out" strategy if you start disagreeing too much, and set some parameters ahead of time (budget, items you're interested in, types of colors and styles and priorities). I usually shop online, but for sofas, I like to go in person with my husband—he's more bullish on making sure the sofa is super comfortable, so I want to make sure I have his buy-in from the beginning. I often steer him toward a curated set of products I like design-wise, and then let him choose the one that he finds the most comfortable. It's also fun to pick things out together that are so important to us as we spend a lot of time chilling on our sofa!

BE OPTIMISTIC THAT THERE WILL BE DESIGN CHALLENGES THAT YOU'LL SOLVE. My husband went to Duke University. Why is this important to note here? Well, if you know anyone who went to Duke, you know that they have a lot of . . . art stuff that is very Duke-centric, and in particular, a lot of stuff regaling Duke's basketball program. You know what that doesn't always fit in with? My glam design style.

My husband has an oil painting of Austin Rivers making the epic game-winning three-point shot against Chapel Hill in February 2012 (his words, not mine) that he did not want to let go of when we moved in together. And you know what? That oil painting makes him so happy, so I didn't want to get rid of it either! I just wanted to make sure that it wasn't prominently featured on our mantel like he initially suggested.

I approached it as a challenge—how can I even incorporate this stuff into my design style? We ended up hanging the oil painting on a gorgeous gallery wall that we have in our entryway. That way it still got decent real estate in our apartment but wasn't hanging up on top of our fireplace in the living room. It camouflaged well with the other pieces on the gallery wall. Win-win!

LEAN INTO WHAT YOU HAVE IN COMMON. Maybe both of you like clean lines. Maybe both of you are drawn to bold colors. Use the things that you know that you both like (and I promise, there are some) to be the unifying factor amongst your design styles.

A good example is one of our original couples at Havenly—Neha and Matt (names changed to protect the innocent). Neha loved patterns and colors. She had a decided preference for more ornate shapes, and was definitely not a minimalist (she joked that she never met an "objet" she didn't love). Matt, on the other hand, was inspired by the *Mad Men* set—low-slung mid-century modern furniture with a heavy preference for clean masculine lines and colors.

What they realized is they liked a bold statement color. They invested in a black leather Chesterfield sofa, accented the room with bold-patterned chairs and rugs, and used the playfulness of color and pattern to dress up the modern shapes that they picked for the foundational pieces for the room.

BE NICE. This may be obvious, but let me clarify what I mean. In our little family, I'm clearly the design person—I mean, I started a design company! It may be easy to ignore my partner's opinions because I'm the one in the know, or I'm the one that cares the most. But the reality is, like everything else you do with your spouse or partner, it's important to actually value the other person's perspective. That may sometimes mean you don't get to achieve your sole vision, but it's worth it when you realize your significant other feels really comfortable in the home that you're creating with them. After all, your shared home is the foundation of your life together.

PART III

STYLING

LIVING ROOM

THERE CAN NEVER BE TOO MANY PILLOWS

Throw pillows can totally change the look of a room, so I hoard them. I even change pillows out seasonally, in some rooms, to add different kinds of flair. My husband isn't a fan; he always removes my artfully arranged pillows, complaining there are too many for him to comfortably sit—but even he acknowledges that they make our place feel "done."

The key to pillows is mixing and matching colors, textures, and patterns. You want to create a totally finished feeling with variation, so that nothing feels too same-same. I know that given the number of pillow choices on the market, it can feel overwhelming to find the perfect combination of cushions, but we're here to help.

HOW TO GROUP PILLOWS

23" square   20" square   18" square   16" square   13"x21" lumbar

As a general rule of thumb, start by arranging your largest pillows at the back of the sofa or at anchor points (the sides near the arms, or the corner of a sectional), and gradually decrease in size as you layer forward. Place the largest pillows as anchors (22 inches square) in the back and add in a layer with a smaller 18- to 20-inch pillow. Fill in with one pillow that isn't square, like an elongated lumbar pillow or rectangular boudoir pillow to create some different levels.

Another thing to consider as you're curating your pillow collection is that if you have one statement pillow (a pillow that has a brighter color, more texture, or more patterns), use the other pillows to pull out key colors, almost as you would do when designing a room around a rug. Add in solid pillows with great textures to balance out the statement of your primary pillow; that way not all of your pillows are competing for the spotlight.

In the living room pictured on pages 200–201, you can see an example of how we combined different pillows for one living room. We started with the larger pillows, which are in shades of blush and neutrals and a few different textures. Then we added some smaller contrasting pillows in front, with varying colors, using the rich ochre as a unifying element. It looks effortless, but the thematic similarity works well to make everything feel collected.

If you want to mix patterns: When mixing patterns, make sure that the sizes of the patterns do not compete with each other. Consider mixing one large pattern, one smaller pattern, and either a solid or a mid-range pattern. If you look at your pillows from a distance and can't tell the patterns apart, they're likely too similar, and you should swap one of them out for a larger (or smaller) pattern instead.

If you want to go minimal: If patterns aren't your thing and you're looking for more of a monochromatic look, use textures to your advantage. Instead of all velvet pillows, throw some linen pillows and a chunky wool lumbar into the mix, and you'll find your vignette looking far more cohesive and interesting than if all your pillows are in the same fabric or texture.

In general, I really don't love pillow groupings that are too similar in color, so I don't get too hung up on ensuring my pillows are all the same shade, and

I don't think you should either. Yes, your pillows (along with your whole room) should share a complementary color palette, but like so many other things in design, you want to avoid feeling too matchy with your pillow choices. Instead, bring in different shades, or adjacent colors, to avoid the matchy-matchy look that can make your space feel less elegant.

Our favorite combinations use pillows that have some movement in the pattern; for example, pillows that have geometric patterns such as stripes or squares; pillows with solid colors; and something with some texture.

SOME COMBINATIONS WE LOVE:

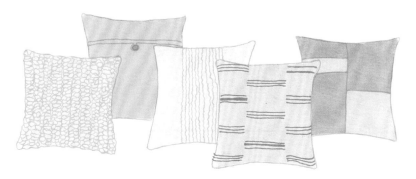

Neutral pillows with different textures—for example, some with cozy, chunky detailing, some in a casual linen weave, and a few that are embroidered for detail and contrast.

Colorful preppy pillows in high-contrast complementary colors—for example, a solid blue pillow with white trim and a pillow with a banana leaf image—offset by a pillow with pink patterns.

Pops of color and pattern mixed with neutral pillows—for example, organic linen pillows in a cream or beige mixed with black-and-blue-patterned pillows.

COFFEE-TABLE STYLING
CAN MAKE THE ROOM

So you've found the perfect coffee table, it works beautifully with your sofa, it's just the right shape and color, and now you're wondering how to get it to look like it's out of a magazine. A bare coffee table, when done intentionally, can be a strong style statement—but otherwise, you're going to want to finish off your space by thinking about how to style the table and make it look like a part of your design. It's the center of your living room, after all.

Consider the clutter factor: How many of you have tried to put together the perfect coffee-table styling, only to have it look like a hodgepodge of objects? I've been there. When this happens, the first consideration is whether the rest of your furniture in conjunction with your coffee-table styling is creating visual clutter. For example, if you have a lot of oversized furniture in the room, consider going minimal with your coffee-table styling. A simple display would be perfect, perhaps add one oversized bowl or an arrangement of large books.

Work with the rule of three: We've talked about the rule of three before, but for coffee tables, you'll use it by mentally dividing your coffee table into three sections (particularly if you have a round coffee table) to plan against. Fill each of the three sections with groups of items with diverse heights and widths to create a "designed"-feeling coffee table.

You can also use the rule of three to think about groupings of items. Group your items in threes (or another odd number) to create arrangements that are pleasing to the eye.

START WITH A STATEMENT PIECE. What's the most interesting thing you want on your table? I love stacks of books, but on some of my coffee tables, I have large earthenware bowls or an oversized candle. I place the statement piece in one of my sections.

ARRANGE COLORS TO COMPLEMENT YOUR STATEMENT PIECE. You don't have to stick to one color, but arranging in a color scheme will help you create a coffee-table arrangement that looks cohesive.

WEAVE IN VARYING HEIGHTS ON YOUR COFFEE-TABLE ARRANGEMENT. Add in a tray to hold some objects, then layer in a tall vase or sculptural element and then a mid-level stack of books. Candles and greenery can complete the look. The idea is to not have too many objects on any horizontal plane, so mix in a lot of heights and varying silhouettes to make the arrangement feel collected but not boring.

USE SOMETHING MEANINGFUL TO YOU. I always like to work in something that has a little bit of story behind it to help a space feel personal—whether it's a book or a special trinket you picked up on that last-minute weekend trip a few months ago.

BOOKSHELVES AREN'T
JUST FOR BOOKS

I've always been a book hoarder, although with all the moving around I did in my twenties, I didn't quite get to a place where I felt as if I had my books artfully displayed in my home. When we first started Havenly, one of our designers was appalled at the state of my built-ins; honestly, they were poorly styled and full of a happy mish mash of . . . books.

I gave her free rein to restyle my shelves, and I learned a lot in the process. She methodically removed all of my books and laid them out on the floor by color (apparently my "theme + alphabetized" method wasn't doing my decor any favors). She then removed a number of book jackets to reveal beautiful hardcover spines: even my Harry Potter books looked adult, very intellectual, and very lovely with their black spines embossed with gold letters.

She then started to work through a color scheme, creating a unified but lived-in feel to my built-ins. She also asked me the hard questions that led to my editing out books and items that weren't in keeping with the theme for display or storage elsewhere. In the end, despite her heavy editing, the built-ins didn't feel sterile. We kept in mementos that were important to me, and by mixing

BOOKS!

The key to styling nearly everything? Coffee-table books. Coffee-table books can help add color or ground accessories to create a polished look. They vary in size and scale, but they share one thing—they are gorgeous inside and out.

Stack your books together and use them as a base for gold accents or a white vase with colorful flowers. The combinations are endless here. I'm a big fan of picking books you actually like to read yourself or that maybe reflect some element of your life or hobbies. On one of my coffee tables, I have a beautiful book about Calcutta, which is where my parents were born, and a book about 200 strong women, reflecting my passion for supporting women in business.

placements and an organic-feeling use of elements, she made my built-ins look stunning. They were functional and organized but had a lot of my personality shining through, and they looked designed.

HERE'S WHAT I LEARNED

Maybe this is obvious, but to style a bookshelf, you probably want to start with . . . books! Books are the most important part of your bookshelf, and you can think of them as the masonry on which to build your shelf styling. Finding the right books and using them to create those anchor points among the shelving is the critical foundation for your entire display so it's important to start off on the right foot. Start by identifying the books—ideally, a mix of books that really reflect your personality but are chosen with a nod to the aesthetics of the bookshelf.

Just like any other space in your house, you'll need to make decisions around the color scheme. I like to do this after I look at my books, so I can create something that feels coordinated and, also, so I'm not buying books just to make the colors look good together. Use books you have and love, that's the whole point of books, and even if you need to adjust to create balance around your favorites, it'll be worth it when you have a bookshelf full of tomes you love. Regardless, giving some thought to color is a good place to start. Ask yourself first whether you want a monochromatic look, something that feels organic and neutral, or bright pops of color throughout. Keeping a consistent color palette is a surefire way to end up with styling that's truly in sync with the rest of your room. If you want to go with a monochromatic color palette, you can take the book jackets off of your hardcover books, which will immediately create consistency and the look of a very stately bookshelf.

Once you've selected books you think are contenders for display, start to arrange your books in horizontal and vertical groupings, varying the size of your book stacks. Stack larger books in groups of two to four books, lean some books against the bookshelf frame itself, and use decorative objects as bookends to anchor smaller books and keep them upright.

Minimalist   Layered   Bibliophile

PRO TIP: For a fuller look, bring the books to the front edge of the shelf rather than pushing them to the back.

You can also make decisions on how full you'd like your styling to be. A more spare look can really suit a clean and modern home, but don't be afraid to create an eclectic feel by taking a more is more approach. Above are some diagrams that show the same three shelves styled with different levels of fullness. You can see that all the styles look collected and designed, so consider how the different styling levels will look given the rest of your room, but also decide how much you'd like to display. If you're a book collector, or you have a lot of interesting objects you'd like to show off, fill them up!

Once you have your books in place, start adding in decorative objects. This is another area where you'll want to mix in some diverse pieces to visually fill the space with items that you may already have that are meaningful to you—a piece of pottery you've inherited from your mother, or a piece of art from your trip to the flea market. The key to starting to place decor in your bookshelves is to place your largest objects first and use them as anchors for the rest of your shelf styling. Maybe your coffee-table-size books are the largest pieces, or maybe you have some large vases or artwork. Don't be afraid to try an arrangement, and then try something else; styling a bookshelf can take some time and experimentation to get right, like one giant puzzle. But a beautiful one!

Once you have your biggest items, create small groupings with your remaining vases and objects and begin placing them on the shelves. Remember to vary the height and the number of objects in each grouping. Mix textures and layers to create a bookshelf that feels as though it's been a part of the house since the day you moved in.

Finally, take a step back and make adjustments until you have a balance of color, texture, and material across the entire shelving unit. Don't be surprised if, like me, you keep tinkering, it's okay to keep it fresh! Take a look at the opposite page and our reasoning below.

1. We selected hardcover books and removed their book jackets to create a more consistent look for the books. We found enough hardcover books to have between three and nine books on each shelf, depending on the size of the display. Then we selected the books that fit the color theme—in this case, the space is very neutral, so we looked for neutral books with black spines.

2. We distributed book groups amongst shelves. We tried out a few arrangements. In this case, we had groups of three or four books stacked, and on other shelves, arranged four to six books vertically. In some cases we added bookends as a fun accent piece that was also practical. In a neutral arrangement like this one, I also like to lean books. We are a reading family, and it creates a little bit of that lived-in feel.

3. We used taller items to fill the shelves. I love putting art (if it fits) on a few of the shelves, but you can also substitute tall vases. By mixing a few frames and sizes, and leaning the frame casually against the wall, you create a fun and organic structure for the remaining objects on your shelf.

4. For a neutral arrangement like this one, use a little bit of greenery (perhaps a succulent plant) or wooden accent items to create a sense of the organic.

Havenly opened a retail store in Boston last summer which you can see on pages 212–213, and really wanted to bring whimsy into the space through styling. The store itself was tiny, only 300 square feet, so we decided to go overtly playful as we decorated our bookshelves. Believe it or not, companies that sell you books by the square foot actually exist—and we used them here. We grouped the books by color, leaving variation among them with different shades of the same color. We then accented each book grouping with gold accessories and earthenware that complemented the dominant color on each shelf. For example, we paired baby pink vases with green books with gold embossing. As a result, the bookshelf is totally different; it really conveys a fun, summery vibe.

FIREPLACE MANTELS THAT YOU'LL WANT TO CURL UP IN FRONT OF

We love ourselves a great mantel. It's a perfect place to showcase a few items, but you also want to keep the styling clean enough so it doesn't feel cluttered. The mantels that fail often feel like a haphazard collection of knickknacks instead of a way to highlight an important decorative accent in a room.

I think a mantel's design should center around a dominant focal element. This is ultimately what you'll want to center your other decorative elements around. The main focal element doesn't have to be just one thing; it can be an arrangement of mirrors, for example. Sometimes people will use their favorite piece of art and in some cases people will use their TV. In most typical living room arrangements, this is the item that the eye will rest on as you're sitting on the sofa in front of the fireplace. I personally love fireplaces that have vintage mirrors, or large-scale pieces of art arranged above the mantel. It adds drama, and it's a lot more visually interesting than a TV. However if watching TV is critical to the function of your room, a TV may be the only option. As you arrange other items on your mantel, just make sure that the quantity or scale of your items don't overwhelm your main piece.

At right, you can see our client Anna's living room mantel, and how she worked with her designer to thoughtfully incorporate a number of elements for a layered look that doesn't at all feel cluttered. She started with the vintage-feeling mirror, and then added a few additional pieces of art, and some photos to make it personal. She brought in greenery elements, and some differing heights with the tapers set in crystal candleholders. All in all, it feels personal but also international.

To make things simple in our great room, since the TV usually takes up so much of the space in the room, we created two arrangements on either side of the mantel. One side of the mantel has books and some decorative objects, and on the other side, we add in some variations in height with candles, balanced out by gold decorative accessories. Personally, I'm glad my designer didn't make me hide my TV—it's a great room, and we're going to watch TV there, so I wanted to make it functional—but still styled.

BEDROOM

PRETEND A DESIGNER MADE YOUR BED

I love to start with a white sheet set as a base. You can invest in nicer white linens because you know it's a classic that will last. But how do you style your bed appropriately?

START WITH THE FLAT SHEET. I personally like to lay the flat sheet on the fitted sheet with some extra at the top edge to fold over either onto itself or over your duvet and blanket.

LAYER ON THE COZY. Add in a quilt and a duvet on top of your sheets. Our favorite way to make the bed is to layer the duvet and then fold it back toward the foot of the bed. Add a throw beneath the folded-back portion—between the sheet and the duvet—to make the bed look irresistibly inviting. You can also fold the duvet into thirds at the foot of the bed or fold it a third of the way back and layer the quilt on top.

SELECT YOUR PILLOWS. You want each person who sleeps in the bed to have at least two sleeping pillows. On a full or queen bed, this will mean two stacks of two standard pillows each at the head of the bed. For a king-size bed, make sure you're using king-size pillows so that they don't look too small at the head of the bed (standard pillows are typically less wide, so if you do want to use standard pillows on a king bed, consider doing three stacks of pillows).

Then you want to choose some throw pillows to add some layers to the bed. Similar to choosing throw pillows for your living room, you'll want to create a complementary but not overly matchy combination to accent your bedroom decor. What you're trying to create is a look so inviting, it welcomes you to dive into the pillows and relax completely.

SOME OF MY FAVORITE ARRANGEMENTS THAT DON'T OVERLOAD THE BED WITH PILLOWS BUT ADD COZINESS AND COMFORT:

A LAYERED LOOK

This is a very symmetrical combination, and is something we come back to often because it's pretty much foolproof. If you'd like to create a more eclectic feeling, you can add a pillow of contrasting shape or texture behind the forward rectangular pillow.

FULL/QUEEN

- Two or four standard-sized bed pillows stacked on top of one another

- Two large square pillows for height (24–26″ square)

- OPTIONAL: Two slightly smaller throw pillows (20–22″ square) in a different shade or pattern

- One smaller rectangular-shaped pillow (14x22″ rectangle) with still another shade or pattern (or consider texture)

KING

- Two or four king-sized bed pillows stacked on top of one another

- Three large square pillows for height (24–26″ square)

- OPTIONAL: Two slightly smaller throw pillows (20–22″ square)

- One smaller rectangular-shaped pillow (14x22″ rectangle)

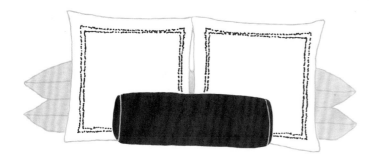

A HOTEL INSPIRED LOOK

There's probably a more technical term for this, but for me this look evokes the joy of melting into a luxurious bed in an upscale hotel. It features crisp, clean white sheets with solid trim to create a really classic feel.

FULL/QUEEN

- Two or four standard-sized bed pillows stacked on top of one another

- Two standard or European shams (we prefer white with solid trim)

- One smaller rectangular-shaped pillow (14x20" rectangle or similar) or boudoir/bolster pillow

KING

- Two or four king-sized bed pillows stacked on top of one another

- Two European shams (we prefer white with solid trim)

- One smaller rectangular-shaped pillow (14x22" rectangle or similar) or boudoir/bolster pillow

A CASUAL LOOK

FULL/QUEEN

- Two or four standard-sized bed pillows stacked on top of one another

- Mix and match four to five different pillows with different but complementary colors and patterns in a variety of sizes. (Try one 26" square, one or two 22–24" square, one 20" square, and a rectangular pillow in front.)

KING

- Two or four king-sized bed pillows stacked on top of one another

- Mix and match four to five different pillows with different complementary colors and patterns in a variety of sizes. (Try one 26" square, one or two 22–24" square, one 20" square, and a rectangular pillow in front.)

CREATING A BEDSIDE TABLE THAT DOESN'T LOOK CLUTTERED

Bedside tables have long been known as the catchall space for late-night snacks, alarm clocks, books, and magazines. But what if there were a way to reorganize this highly valuable bedroom real estate so that it could be both functional *and* stylish? We have some ideas for you.

1. **SCENTED CANDLES.** Having a scented candle on your bedside table is an absolute must as far as we're concerned. It's the perfect way to de-stress after a long day's work and helps soothe your mind so that you can peacefully fall asleep. We have a major obsession when it comes to Diptyque candles. The brand is a bit more expensive, but each scent has a 72-hour burning time, which is higher than the standard candle. If you're new to the brand, we highly recommend Feu de Bois. It has a sophisticated blend of rare woods, which is the perfect scent when we approach the colder seasons.

2. **BOOKS.** We're the type of people who think reading a good book is an essential part of a nightly routine. I personally find that it helps calm my mind and focus my attention before sleep. Your bedside table will happily hold neatly stacked smaller books, and they can function as a decorative element too, particularly when topped with a small vase of fresh flowers or a candle.

3. **JEWELRY DISHES.** Having a jewelry dish on your bedside table is essential if you love to accessorize and wait until you get into bed before you remove your jewelry. The dish will give your jewelry a safe, organized place to land at night because there's nothing worse than waking up with an earring tangled in your hair. Been there, done that!

4. **FRESH FLORALS.** Flowers are the perfect addition to any bedside table. Hydrangeas and peonies are my go-to flowers during the summertime, and garden roses take that spot come winter. If you'd prefer something a little more long lasting, consider a succulent (not one that's excessively thorny to avoid accidental injury) or greenery as well. Flowers bring life to your bedside table and can help cheer up a simple arrangement if you have a smaller nightstand.

HOME OFFICE

Home offices have been a hot topic for so many of us recently, as more of us have started to work flexibly, which often means answering emails and taking calls from home. In the past, home offices have been an afterthought for me, but now that working from home is more of the norm, I've really thought about upgrading my setup. A primary consideration for a home office is just ensuring there's some amount of separation from other living spaces, and that it's actually usable (comfortable, well lit, with plenty of storage). This is one area of the house where you really want function to reign supreme over style.

GET SEPARATED. Many of us don't have designated spaces for our work areas, so carving out space from an existing space is necessary. Given you don't always have the luxury of a dedicated room for your home office, figuring out how to create a little bit of separation between work and life is not just a good styling suggestion but a good, practical one. Not only will that mean you can take work calls in peace, it'll also help you transition after a long workday. For people who are carving out space for their office from their bedrooms or living rooms, think about potentially adding in a folding screen in a neutral fabric to separate out the spaces. Or convert an underused closet into an office area by removing the door and door trim and adding in a built-in desk.

STORAGE MATTERS. Whether your office is a separate room or not, clutter is not your friend here. Messy piles of paper do not just affect how the space looks visually, but it really does make it more difficult to relax and focus. Create some order in the chaos, and invest in organization. Buy bins with closed tops so you can hide away files in a semiorganized fashion into appropriate places, without adding a lot of extra work.

MOTIVATION THROUGH DECOR. If you're going to be sitting in your home working, shouldn't it at least inspire you to be your best you? What's motivating about blah gray walls and a home office in the back corner of the basement? The answer obviously, is nothing. Brighten it up! This is an area where you want tons of light (if you can't find a place with sunny natural light, paint your walls a bright color that's sure to cheer you up). It's also an area where you want the big interesting piece of art and fun wallpaper. Get some good task lighting, and you're all set to tackle the day (and look good on Zoom, to boot).

PLAY UP COMFORT. Again, I once thought that I could survive on backless barstools for the amount of time I work from home. It turns out, if you spend any more than an hour on those stools, you'll be in for some serious back pain. Get a chair that really works. Forget about the aesthetics (although if you can afford a sleeker look with support, go for it), and really maximize your budget for the most comfy chair you can find. But don't stop at the chair—pull in a cozy rug, if you have space for it, and add some cozy accent seating where you can take some of those video calls.

DINING ROOM

MAKE THE DINING TABLE DINNER PARTY WORTHY

Excited to channel your inner Ina Garten and throw a casual but elegant dinner party in your home? Up your dinner party game by styling your dining room like a pro. Like many other parts of your home, you want to think about the look you are going for with your dining table. Do you want something a little more minimal and clean (and easier to keep up) or are you looking to do a cozier layered chic look?

If you like a softer, more layered look (think Hamptons chic), I recommend that you start with linens. A tablecloth or a table runner can add texture and pattern and provide the backdrop for everything that will come next. You can also play with linens to create a look that's less expected. Rather than laying the tablecloth straight on top of the table, turn a square tablecloth 45 degrees from the lines of the table to create contrasting angles. Rather than laying a table runner down the length of your table, lay multiple runners across the narrower width of the table so that the two seats across from each other share a runner. Layering cloths and runners also helps add texture and contrast. When choosing the fabric, consider linen or cotton as it always seems appropriate for any season or occasion, and is easier to clean.

There's nothing wrong with a bare table, though. If you'd rather keep your tables more modern or minimal (or you're afraid of spills and mess), you can skip the table linens. You can still add interest and softness with napkins, flower arrangements, and other accessories. An intentionally unadorned table, particularly if the overall room has modern styling, can be a strong decor statement, as well.

CREATE A FOCAL POINT

Almost all tables should have some table styling, and we recommend even the most minimal dining tables have some sort of a centerpiece on the table. It can be simple: vases, bowls, urns, candles, and flowers are a great place to start with your centerpiece. If you're going with multiple items, choose elements that create different horizontal planes by varying the height of the objects. However, ensure that you're not choosing anything too tall in the center of the table to avoid impeding conversation across the table. Remember to mix and match finishes between the items you choose for your centerpiece, and ensure some contrast between those finishes and that of the dining table itself. For example, you can combine natural elements such as driftwood bread bowls, or potted succulents with glass bowls, metal candlesticks, and mirrored finishes. You'll want to make sure there's a little bit of contrast on the table, so if your table is oak, all of your decorative elements shouldn't also be wood. Don't be afraid to extend your centerpiece the span of the table length either; it doesn't just have to be one piece in dead center. If you do create a long decorative element, just be sure all of the items are relatively low in height, and repeat elements and arrangements down the table length for a cohesive look.

Vases full of fresh flowers, arrangements of greenery, and gourds are the perfect table centerpiece solution. If you're looking for a repeating arrangement across the length of a table, I'd pick an item that's substantial that you can use as a repeating anchor across the length of the table. Then, fill in the gaps with candlestick holders, smaller flower arrangements, or interesting decor items.

Don't forget to leave room for the food. If you need to go more minimal, either for functional and space reasons or because you like a more clean look, a simple, pretty arrangement of fruit in the center of the table can also be sublime.

MAKE THE PLACE SETTINGS SING

Your place settings don't have to be formal to look upscale and elegant. Keep your cabinets stocked with simple staples such as white dishware and simple but refined glassware, and add some flair with accessory items and linens. Napkins are a great opportunity to add color and pattern into your tablescape. A trend we love is gold- and brass-toned flatware and glassware that provide a contemporary update to a formal setting and can make your table feel festive on special occasions.

Unsure how to style your napkins? Here are three ideas:

1. This one is my favorite option because my linens are never pressed (who has time to iron napkins?). Take opposing corners of your napkin and fold it diagonally. Take a corner and twist the rest into a long ropelike shape. Then use a napkin ring to hold it in place.

2. You can't go wrong with a classic trifold placed on the topmost plate in your setting. Place the silverware on top of the napkin for a timeless look.

3. Fold your napkin long-ways into thirds for a thin rectangular shape. Lay the napkin under the bottom-most dish and allow the napkin to drape off of the table.

Some people love chargers, and I happen to be one of those people. For my formal dining room, depending on the season, I'll lay out either wood or metallic chargers to add another decorative layer to my table that guests nearly always appreciate. I just think chargers help make the setting feel more substantial, but it is a matter of personal taste. Again, if you're looking for a more minimal feel, you can always skip this component.

Don't forget your serving dishes! Serveware can also be critical to dining table styling, but hopefully also practical, so make sure you stock an array of shapes and sizes to accommodate all of your delicious eats. I personally like to buy serveware that features natural materials like bamboo, wood, and terra cotta for an artisan look, but a simple white serving dish can do wonders. Whether you're hosting a dinner party or just serving dinner to the family, serveware can totally double as decor, and hopefully highlight all the food you spent hours cooking (but we don't judge, it can also make takeout look good!).

ACCESSORIZE

The last, and perhaps most enjoyable, step of decorating your table is accessorizing. Napkin rings, place cards, menus, or small gifts are quick and inexpensive ways to jazz up your table decor in a personal way. Top your plates with season-appropriate, nature-inspired decor or tie your napkins with a place card and some twine so that there are no awkward "Where should I sit?" moments when your guests arrive. If you're feeling particularly generous, a small homemade gift atop each place setting at a dinner party adds a lovely decorative touch and is always a thoughtful way to thank your guests for leaving the comfort of their own homes to share a meal with you.

Glassware is a go-to when you're looking for creative ways to bring your tablescape to life. I always accessorize with simple classics: a water glass in simple blown glass, a long-stemmed thin-rimmed Zalto wineglass. But don't be afraid to choose something with a little more personality. One of our in-house designers swears by her vintage-inspired, mismatched, ornate wineglasses, because she feels like they add a cozy and eclectic touch to an otherwise simple table.

Lighting is a key part of accessorizing your dining table that you don't want to overlook. For instance, when you install lights in your dining room, use dimmers so that you can moderate the harshness of the light, after all, you do not want your lovely dinner party to evoke memories of a harshly lit cafeteria! Play up the drama by going big on candles. Candles in dining rooms are everything. Really. You can do simple tea lights for an inexpensive but romantic look, or tapers set in candleholders for that classic elegance. To create variation, use candles with different heights grouped together to create levels and give your table more of an organic look.

Some tabletop mixing ideas:

A plaid tabletop runner with black matte silverware, wood serving platters and chargers, and gold-rimmed white flatware. This is a festive but not cheesy look for holiday entertaining.

A natural linen runner with abundant greenery for centerpieces is a great match with wooden chargers and artisanal flatware. Combine this with elegant white tapers in earthenware candleholders for a lush but eclectic-feeling table.

Or for a very festive look try red tapers in gold candleholders with a blush-and-white tablecloth-and-runner combination, and lush pink-and-red flowers for centerpieces. Pair this with white-and-cream earthenware and blush pink accents, along with gold utensils, to create a feminine and romantic tablescape.

OTHER DINING ROOM STYLING TIPS

Find stylish storage. If you have room for it, I think every dining room could use an extra space to store your dining ware and to create a little bit more real estate to serve meals. We like the look of a long and low sideboard or buffet to add closed storage for your linens and plates when they're not in use. You can also style the buffet much as you would a coffee table for another place to express your personality in the dining room.

Some options to decorate your sideboard include:

A matching pair of lamps, with a large mirror hanging centered above the buffet

A set of larger-scale paintings leaning against the wall, with greenery accents

A large painting hung a few inches above the sideboard, with three different levels of decorative accessories placed on the sideboard.

SERVE DRINKS WITH FLAIR

Bar carts are the secret to a great dinner party, and we strongly believe a good host has her bar cart game locked down. Why do we love bar carts, you ask? Because bar carts are versatile, beautiful, stylish, and functional. And if those reasons aren't enough, then this one ought to seal the deal: bar carts are *EASY!*

Whether you're styling a bar cart as a finishing touch to your living or dining room design or are just whipping up a quick bar scene for a get-together, spend some time creating a beautiful bar cart, and your guests will be impressed.

Some bar cart ideas:

1. Add a tray and shaker. This isn't just because they're pretty. The shaker adds height to your visual landscape while being an important cocktail making tool, and the tray creates a strong visual but also serves to corral your drinkware.

2. Insert plenty of stylish drinkware. Don't forget: bar carts are magic. They serve their function as much as they honor their style. So when your stash of drinkware isn't being used to serve your guests, it will serve to create a gorgeous bar cart vignette that's nothing less than eye candy.

3. Add color with reusable metal straws, fruit, and stir sticks. Your bar cart ought to include everything you might need to make a party drink. An occasional trip to the fridge for ice is acceptable, but don't make your guests go rooting around in your kitchen drawers for cocktail accoutrements. Keep your bar well stocked and stylish: lemons, limes, and cherries add some much-needed pops of color, and olives in a glass bowl will add a touch of sophistication.

4. Collect your booze. It's worth spending a little extra effort to source bottles and cans that look great. In short, select only the prettiest liquors to put on display. So skip the generic Jack Daniels bottle (or keep it hidden inside a cabinet), and instead display pretty liquors and higher-end wines to create some interest.

5. Don't forget the tools of the cocktail trade. Make sure you have a place to muddle that lime! Your bar cart is only as strong as the drinks you can serve from it. Style with a mortar and pestle, coasters, and any other tools you might need to mix it up.

6. Finish with art. The cart alone is a work of art. That said, if you've placed your cart up against a wall, you'll likely want to fill in that empty space above it with a piece of art to complete the picture.

MAKE ACCESSORIZING PERSONAL (AND SHOP YOUR HOME)

There's nothing like having an empty bookshelf that you get to style. Okay, fine—for most of us, it's actually a little stressful to think about styling a bookshelf or a coffee table, but for me, reminding myself that it's more important that it makes me happy helps to put things into context. Your accessorizing, from art to knickknacks, could and should really hold meaning. That's how you make your house your home.

SHOWCASE ART THAT YOU LOVE

Don't be afraid to break the mold with art. I think this is the item in your home where you really want it to say something about you, or what you like. That doesn't always mean picking out art that you love from expensive artists but really that you get creative in finding things that reflect an interesting part of your (or your family's) story.

Some of my favorite ways to get creative when choosing art that is beyond "a pretty picture":

- Art that represents a city or area that is important to you. I have a piece of art that shows Kolkata, where my family is from, hanging in my bedroom

- An image or portrait that is a hand-me-down from family members. Our head of design, Shelby, has a portrait of her grandmother hanging in her Brooklyn dining room.

- Consider framing your kids' art. Lee's two boys painted some large-scale abstract work with black-and-white watercolor that she got framed for their bedrooms.

- Pick up art on your travels. There's no better way to remember an amazing vacation than having a unique piece of art to commemorate that time.

FRAME EVERYTHING

We're used to framing photos or art, but nowadays, a lot of online framers will frame mementos and other items. I know a lot of my friends have framed wedding invites or ketubahs that grace their walls. But I've even seen clients frame matchbooks from the restaurants in which they had their first few dates, or plane tickets to their favorite vacations. Don't be afraid to get creative here, and really bring some life into the space.

DISPLAY ECLECTIC THINGS (WITHIN REASON)

I love how found items from travels and life bring interest into a space. I love displaying the handcrafted throw that I picked up at a market in Dubai and juxtaposing that with some candles that were left over from my days in Nashville. It's okay to mix and match with your accents to bring a really personal touch to your home.

The big thing here is that if you display mementos and souvenirs, the look and feel of your room will continue to change as you have more life and travel experiences. It's such a wonderful and organic feeling to have your home evolve just as you do.

PRO TIP: Use trays to keep your mementos organized and provide a uniform backdrop for your souvenirs. Trays can be a great way to accent your treasured finds but also can keep things looking more intentional and less cluttered.

BOOKS AND BOOKS

What better way to show your personality than displaying books that you actually love. Yes, I know, in all of the home magazines, there are books that are displayed because they're pretty. But if you have books that have meaning, or history, or even just ones that you really love to read, show them off. Arrange the books in visually interesting ways, as we talk about in this chapter, and you'll be able to combine function, personality, and design.

BATHROOM

Bathrooms can be tricky. They're the one room in the house in which your guests are guaranteed to spend some time alone. Oftentimes, a full renovation of an underwhelming bathroom is out of budget, but you can make some inexpensive changes to make it feel luxurious and, dare I say, even fun.

THINK ABOUT FLOOR COVERINGS. Hate your contractor-grade tile, but don't want a renovation? We love adding rugs to warm up the room and take the focus away from the tile. While bath mats are certainly an option in smaller bathrooms, a larger luxurious rug (even an antique one) makes the room feel more homey and generally adds personality to a boring bathroom.

UPGRADE THE SOFT STUFF. Clean, fluffy towels and a clean shower curtain can do wonders for even the most depressing bathrooms. This might be a no-brainer, but no one wants to see the faded towels that you've had for the last twenty years. New towels are an inexpensive upgrade to make. I usually gravitate toward white linens because they remind me of a hotel and they are easy to clean with bleach. You can even have a shower curtain or a roman shade made from white linen to complement the rest of the room and make it feel cohesive.

BRING IN PRETTY SCENTS. You can never go wrong adding fresh flowers or candles (and matches) to a bathroom. The smells and florals can make a room feel tended-to and pretty. Decorative touches like a candle or a fresh bowl of flowers are perfect ways to incorporate color into your bathroom styling as well. They can serve as your main decorative element if you have a smaller bathroom.

GET CREATIVE. When you have that itch to do something different from the rest of your house, the bathroom is a great place to explore your creative side. It's a small room, so if something goes terribly wrong, it's not too expensive to fix, and you can be a bit more daring given the look will be visible only in relatively small doses. Add a vibrant patterned wallpaper or dark paint scheme to make the room pop. And to bring drama to the space, you can add a unique lighting fixture or mirror. This is a room where you can go out of your comfort zone. It might really pay off!

WATCH THE LIGHTING. Bathrooms can be tricky for lighting. Too blue or cold, and you get a really harsh fluorescent cast that flatters no one. Too yellow, and the bathroom can look, well, too yellow—which is not a good look for a bathroom. Lighting is an inexpensive upgrade to do if you have a dated or ho-hum bathroom. Replace any fluorescent or tube lighting with recessed lights in the ceiling. Add in wall sconces if you only have overhead lighting to get more accent lighting near the sink and mirror. Consider adding chandeliers if you have a bathtub or a dressing area that needs a focal element.

MAKE IT FEEL LIKE HOME. Consider incorporating a vintage dresser for linen storage or a unique light fixture into your bathroom design. If you can incorporate styles that are dominant in the rest of your home, it can make the bathroom feel as if it's a continuation of the rest of your house. And, no, it's not weird to hang art in your bathroom just as you would in your living room! Treat this room as a small living space, and you and your guests will feel right at home. I've seen everything from personal photographs to original art hung in the bathroom. My favorite bathrooms incorporate a little bit of whimsy, so don't be afraid to break the rules in this room.

CUT THE CLUTTER. Nothing ruins the look of a bathroom like a counter full of medicine, makeup, and toiletries. In bathrooms that get a lot of use from the family, if necessary, add storage, preferably closed; after all, your guests don't need to know which deodorant brand you use. In a guest bathroom or powder room, edit the toiletries mercilessly. You really don't need five canisters of different goodies sitting out. The essentials are hand soap, a cup or toothbrush holder for guests, and a candle and matches. If you have a large space and need some more decor, add pieces sparingly.

BE OUR GUEST. Whether the bathroom you're styling is a guest bathroom or a master bathroom, make sure to add in some luxe amenities. Some ideas include matching bottles of shampoo and conditioner, a white robe and comfy slippers, and even glass jars with helpful sundries such as cotton balls and Q-tips. It will look nice, and your guests will be amazed at the thoughtful touches.

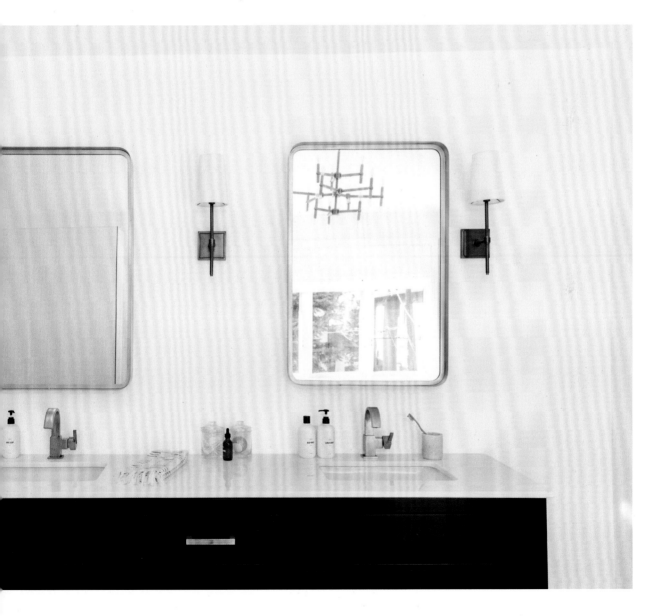

KITCHEN

Not all of us are Martha Stewart in the kitchen, but there's no reason your kitchen can't look just as well designed as the rest of the house. As with bathrooms, sometimes it can be hard to find the time or budget to do kitchen renovations, so think about using styling elements to create an inexpensive upgrade. For me, the key to kitchen styling is the countertop vignette. If you follow any home accounts on Instagram, you've probably seen a lot of beautifully styled kitchens, and you probably also know that you can really use functional ware as decor in a kitchen.

CREATE VIGNETTES. Find a few items with varying heights and materials. I love displaying large rustic-wood cutting boards together with earthenware in odd number combinations. Make sure you place pieces of different heights in front of one another, to create some dimension.

GO SIMPLE. I personally don't think you need to display fancy china, and, in fact, I prefer to show the simpler or more rustic pieces. These days, we're finding more people forgo heritage bone china in favor of simple dishware. I personally like to mix and match whatever I have that's clean. My favorite items to display include a wooden bowl from Amazon near a marble cheese board, with a couple stacks of my favorite everyday white dishware.

USE THE FOOD. I also love that in the kitchen you can use food as styling props. I peel the stickers off my lemons and place them in a bowl for a pop of color or place my weekly parsley stash in a mason jar to add in some inexpensive green (and, it's also delicious).

BOOKS AS PROPS. Another item that you probably have in your kitchen that can double as a styling item? Cookbooks. I have a ton of beautiful hardcover

cookbooks. Arranged on floating shelves or at the ends of counters, the books can be within reach when you want to make a specific recipe but add a bit of functional decoration as well.

KITCHEN TOWELS. I love kitchen towels! I have a whole drawer full of them in various shades of blues and grays. I use them a lot when I'm cooking (I challenged myself this year to cook at home at least four days of the week), and kitchen towels are great for quick cleanups while I'm whipping up something (mostly) delicious. Towels are an inexpensive but easy way to make the kitchen feel lived-in, and add softness to the overall space. Buy a bunch of clean kitchen towels from Target in your favorite color palette for an instant upgrade to your kitchen. Fold them and hang them over the handles of your dishwasher or oven, or just leave them on the counter for an artfully lived-in look.

LIGHTING. When a major kitchen remodel is not doable—either because it's not in your budget or your landlord doesn't have it on the radar—lighting can be a big opportunity to inexpensively change your kitchen's look and feel. In fact, I've used lighting to rescue a few very sad rental apartments, buying inexpensive stick-on under-cabinet lighting and adding some hanging pendants (or changing out my existing pendants). In each case, the added lighting softened up the horrible fluorescent lighting and created some design detail. It was also cheap to replace and easy to remove when my rental contract was over. (Yay, security deposit!)

A LE CREUSET. Yes, yes, I know: there are less expensive versions of these kitchen essentials. But I use my white Le Creuset (previously, I used a red one in a kitchen that needed a pop of color) as art. It really can be a great decorative item that breaks up the monotony of a stovetop. Added bonus: staring at it every day is a good way to get inspired to cook delicious braised meals.

EASY UPGRADES ON DATED SPACES

DINGY ROOM? PAINT THE WALLS

This is the easiest thing to do. (Although, I admit, I hate painting. I once tried to paint my apartment, and quit in the middle of it.) However, a gallon of paint is an inexpensive thing, and with a few cheap brushes, a lot of painter's tape, and a Saturday, you can totally change the look of a place. A fresh coat of white paint on a nondescript greige room can breathe new life into it.

When I look at Lee's place, the biggest difference between the befores and afters (we didn't include the befores because they're alarming) is her painting over the original taupe color with a fresh white, which made the place light and bright. Even in my first apartment in NYC, that was an easy upgrade that I was able to do, which was landlord approved but instantly gave the place a new sparkle (which was important, because as I mentioned before, it was a studio).

CHANGE YOUR LIGHT FIXTURES

This is actually a tip that's great for the renters out there. So many rental apartments (and being a New Yorker, I've lived in a lot of these) have these generic overhead light fixtures—or worse, ceiling fans with lights. (I know many will disagree, but first of all, ceiling fans with lights are NOT a good look.)

In my opinion, this is a great upgrade for a rental, because it's pretty cost effective and easy, and it is also easy to change back! So don't be afraid to replace those "nipple lights" or dated fixtures in your rental with something that's a lot more stylish. It's a great way to add some style to your space.

UGLY KITCHEN? PAINT THE CABINETS

So maybe you inherited a home with mid 1990s wood-toned cabinetry in the kitchen. Or worse, like one of our clients, a mauvy-pink colored cabinet. Paint those too! How do you know if your cabinets will look good with paint? Well, any cabinet material that can be sanded is a prime candidate. But even laminate candidates will work; you just need to get a special bonding primer.

There are lots of guides on how to paint cabinets, but the process is simple (if time consuming, so enlist a friend, and do it over a long weekend). In a nutshell:

• Clean out the drawers and cabinets

• Remove the doors

• Clean the doors and remove grease and dirt, and repair holes

• Sand everything down (for wood)

• Prime and paint

Pro tip: Think about also upgrading dated cabinet hardware for a fresh modern look.

UGLY BATHROOM? SO MANY OPTIONS

Honestly, I think this is an easy room for quick and cheap upgrades. It's typically a smaller room, so if you want to try your hand at DIY projects, it's a good place to start— and there are some easy hacks to create a more pulled-together space. Here are some of my favorite upgrades in a bathroom:

FRAME IN YOUR CONTRACTOR-GRADE MIRROR. If your bathroom has one of those big mirrors with little detailing, buy some wood and some paint and add a frame around the edges to make it look like a higher-end vanity mirror.

COVER UP YOUR TILE WITH INEXPENSIVE BATH MATS OR RUGS. We're a fan of crisp white cotton bath mats or, in a bigger space, using a rug to cover up some of the tile. I actually love using Persian rugs in a bathroom to really make it feel like any other room in your house and pull the space together.

CHANGE OUT YOUR LIGHTS. Does your bathroom have horrendous lighting? An easy upgrade is to either change out just the light bulb (see our discussion on page 45 about lighting colors), or change out the fixtures to something more aesthetically pleasing.

CAULK AROUND THE TUB OR SHOWER. Lee once lived in a walkup in NYC that had a brown, dry, and cracked border around a perfectly serviceable tub. The easiest fix? Caulk it up.

FREQUENTLY ASKED DESIGN QUESTIONS

First, congratulations on getting most of your big pieces right—that's a great place to start. But just like any outfit, your home won't feel done until it's fully accessorized.

Here's what I'd suggest: make sure you actually do have all the foundational pieces you need. Did you buy a rug? Accent chairs or tables? Storage? Do you have layered lighting? If not, make sure that you have all the key components to making your room fully designed.

Avoid the matchy-matchy. If you made the mistake of buying items that are only one-note in color or style, that's okay, you just have to mix things up a bit. In a living room that has too many items in the same shade of blue, try adding pops of black or green, and varying your shades of blue to create contrast. If you've got things that feel too much in the same style note, bring in complementary but thoughtfully curated pieces to create a more "done" feeling.

Accessorize. Look at the small things—can you add in more decorative elements? I love bringing in plants to elevate a space. Make sure you style the tabletops, nightstands and consoles with combinations of coffee-table books and curated objets d'art.

Find art. Fill up those walls—blank ones will always feel a little incomplete unless it's highly intentional, and in keeping with a minimalist look.

I HAVE A BIG BLANK WALL THAT IS JUST SO BLANK, PLEASE HELP!

Okay, this is the fun part. You can really do whatever you want. There are so many options, but I'll list some of my favorites here:

Large-scale art. Find a statement art piece that you love. Art at this scale can be expensive, so consider investing in something that really speaks to you. A few dramatic art pieces can really make a difference in a room. I actually love the look of adding a large piece of art that really complements the room, and then adding a gallery light above the piece for an added emphasis, a bit of a layering, and a touch of elegance.

Gallery walls. Gallery walls continue to be popular, and why shouldn't they be? They are an excellent way to cover space and curate an interesting collection that represents you. Don't be afraid to mix and match frames, art, and other objects to create a look that feels collected but cohesive.

Wallpaper. Add fun wallpaper to bring in some variety. This is especially useful in rooms that don't get used a ton (guest bedrooms, bathrooms), so you won't get sick of the pattern but can go a little bit more spicy than the rest of the house.

Shelving. If your wall is in a space where you might need storage, consider shelving or bookcases. For example, I had a big blank wall in my kitchen, and I bought some wood shelves to display dinnerware. In a living room or study, bookcases can do the trick and also add opportunity to display interesting objects and your favorite books.

SHOULD I BUY THINGS FROM A MATCHING SET?

No. I know a lot of retailers like to run combo sales, and buying a matching set is relatively easy and thus incredibly tempting. But whether it's a bedroom set or outdoor furniture set, just. don't. do. it.

But maybe you already have things from a matching set. It's okay, you can fix this by moving things between rooms or adding in complementary but not fully matching items. For example, if you bought a matching bedroom set, consider moving your nightstands to a guest bedroom and moving the dresser into the kids' playroom.

WHAT ARE YOUR FAVORITE INDOOR PLANTS FOR MY SPACE?

There's nothing like greenery to brighten up a home. Here are some of our favorites:

Fiddle Leaf Fig
Can a tree have an "it" moment? If so, the plant that's really basking in the proverbial Instagram sun is the fiddle leaf fig. With a tall trunk and large and dramatic leaves, this is an elegant option for any well-lit room. This plant needs a lot of sun and weekly watering, so it can still be a little more fickle than other indoor plants. Give it a bit of love, and you'll find it pays back in spades.

Olive Tree
I won't lie, I'm obsessed with my olive tree, even though it doesn't bear fruit indoors. I think it's a tree that adds some color to my neutral dining room without overpowering the space. The ancient olive tree is from the Mediterranean, so it does well indoors, even in drier climates, like Denver, where I live so you don't have to water too frequently.

Rubber Plant
I have rubber plants scattered throughout my house because they're both easy to maintain and lovely to look at, with thick waxy leaves and substantial vertical growth. Rubber plants do also require bright natural light, but they can survive without a lot of water, so if you sometimes forget to water (like me), it's a perfect option.

Bird of Paradise
This tall tropical-looking plant can add a bit of drama to any indoor space. I love the bird of paradise because it reminds me of the banana trees I encountered during my childhood trips to India. Outdoors, these plants bloom with bright wild-looking flowers, but indoors, the plant grows tall with beautiful foliage. These plants are native to tropical regions, so will need constant care to keep the soil and environment moist to grow appropriately.

Snake Tree (Sansevieria)

These plants, with their upright sword- or tongue-like leaves, are extremely easy to care for, and would actually work in low-light situations too. In planters, they make a versatile plant that can top off a dresser, but they also brighten up an unused corner.

WHAT'S THE BIGGEST DESIGN FAUX PAS THAT OTHERWISE STYLISH PEOPLE MAKE?

Honestly, I hate to call anything a faux pas, because if something really works for you, well, you do you. However, there are mistakes that I see in otherwise adorable rooms that sort of hurt my heart because they're simple to fix, but the mistakes really take away from the feel of the room. Once you learn about them, it's hard to not notice them and want to fix them. Here is a list of some of the most frequent little design mistakes we see:

Art hung too high

I was guilty of this until I started working with all the Havenly designers at the office. Art hung too high really is tough to see and doesn't visually tie into a room—it's hard for art to have an impact if you have to stretch to even see the piece! Ideally, art should be hung at eye level, so about 55 to 60 inches above the floor.

If you're hanging art above a sofa, consider placing the bottom edge 6 inches above the top of the sofa. If you're new to hanging art, this may feel strange, but oddly, if you leave too much white space above the furniture item and under the art, the piece feels lost and the arrangement looks a little, well, sad.

If you're placing art on a wall without furniture in a room with 9-foot ceilings, think about placing the vertical center of the art just shy of 5 feet from the floor. Hang it there, and then step back and see how it feels to you, and make adjustments until it's just right.

Rugs that are too small

I'm repeating what I've said in the previous sections about choosing rugs, but it's a common mistake. If you can, try and fit all of your furniture on the rug. If you can't, make sure that at least two legs of all of your furniture can fit on the rug. If it can't all fit, get a bigger rug (or swap out the rug for a larger one you already have).

Art that's too small

Scale really matters with both rugs and art, and while neither is a total deal-breaker, getting the right size art is an easy fix that can instantly elevate a room. If it's too small, it'll look washed out and out of place, and will generally make the wall feel neglected.

A good rule of thumb is to have the art take up about two-thirds of the room of the wall, or two-thirds of the width of the furniture piece it's hung above. (And if you're hanging multiple pieces of art, think of all the pieces together as one large installation.)

Too much matchy-matchy

Again, this isn't always intuitive to most people, so even stylish rooms can suffer from overmatched accessories. Unlike that matching sweatsuit you've been living in all weekend, having too many items in the exact same shade and texture looks unsophisticated and ultimately, boring. Make sure to vary your tones, add adjacent or complementary colors, and add variety with texture to bring that designer feel to any room.

HOW DO I HANG A GALLERY WALL?

A very popular question. I love gallery walls. There's nothing better to bring in personality and add an interesting touch to a room. There are a few schools of thought on how best to hang gallery walls I typically try to eyeball it, but with a larger or more complex arrangement, you can also use the following tips to get it done.

First, make sure you have a pencil, measuring tape, a level, nails/hammer, and command strips, or similar. Then, try and size out where you may want the arrangement on your wall. Remember to make sure that the scale is large enough for the wall and that the overall installation is generally placed appropriately on the wall. When you're thinking about size or scale, follow the rules of thumb for art, but account for the whole gallery wall as one large piece. So the scale of the gallery wall installation should follow the two-thirds rule mentioned at left, for example.

I like to start with the largest piece that you plan to hang first, and I typically put it somewhere in the middle. In order to ensure that you don't hang it too high, think about placing the center of the piece about 57 inches above the floor, or at eye level. If you're hanging the gallery wall above a sofa or other furniture item, you can also start with the piece you intend to hang the lowest, and ensure that the bottom of that piece is 5 to 8 inches above the furniture item, and work your way up and out.

Then you'll want to work around this anchor piece and work your way out (or work your way up, if you started with the "lowest piece"

approach). Keep the frames 2 to 3 inches apart, and make sure that all the pieces have consistent spacing between each other to make everything look intentional.

I typically do this by placing the pieces on the wall and directly hammering in each piece. However, if you're a perfectionist, have an exceptionally large piece, or generally feel uncomfortable, you can also use templates that you make from craft or construction paper. Basically, trace each item onto the paper, and then cut out the outline to form a template. Then you can use painter's tape to arrange them on the wall, for a mess-free way to get everything in the right spot (and try different arrangements).

Once the frames are hung, I use a level to make things straight and use command tape on the backs of the frames to make sure they stay put and all aligned. Seeing a gallery wall that's askew is one of my personal pet peeves, and I've been known to walk into people's offices at Havenly HQ just to straighten the art.

WHAT ARE SOME ORGANIZATIONAL TIPS THAT YOU FIND HELPFUL?

I keep trying to Marie Kondo my house, but I'll admit to holding onto too many things. Also, with two kids at home, and a dog who has a lot of toys, I've found the need for lots of stylish, inexpensive, covered storage. Covered storage is key for our family—it allows us to hide the clutter but not constantly be nagging the kids to clean up. We keep a big storage chest, or storage ottoman, in all of the rooms in which our kids play. This way, the kids can stash things away after they're done playing, and it's a relatively simple task for them. I buy simple white storage chests from Wayfair, which are clean, aren't an eyesore, and are inexpensive. Using catchall bins are great for ad hoc decluttering—but you definitely have to make sure you go through and clear them out every once in a while to ensure they don't get out of control.

In general, though, consider having enough closed storage. I love the look of open shelving, but having enough storage that visually hides away clutter is critical to feeling like your home is organized, but also that lets you avoid constantly straightening up.

Make the most of the inside of storage spaces. I invest in drawer organizers and shelf risers to keep my drawers and vanities from looking super scary. What's the point of drawers if it takes you fifteen minutes to find that one eye shadow or the box of Girl Scout cookies. The Container Store has an endless amount of options, but I use shelf risers liberally to get more vertical space in my cupboards, and use drawer organizers to avoid a jumbled mess.

For papers and important documents, go vertical. We all have a tendency to put papers in piles, but then it's hard to look through, and impossible to easily access. I like to create a vertical filing system—either a filing drawer or just a series of paper organizers stored vertically—so I can easily and visually see where everything is. I also try to digitize everything I can using a scanner app on my phone, so it gets off of my counters.

In smaller homes, think about using vertical space. Want to get the most out of the unused vertical space in your small apartment? Think about building in more storage above you. Consider building shelves above your sofa to store books, or adding in covered storage cabinets at the top of a coat closet. I like to get as much off of my counters as possible, so I'll even use hooks to hang pots and pans next to my cabinets, and add shelves above my bathroom doors to store everyday things like towels and toilet paper.

HOW DO YOU FEEL ABOUT ACCENT WALLS? HOW SHOULD I CHOOSE AN ACCENT WALL?

I think accent walls are a great way to bring color and vibrance into your room, without feeling like you have to commit for all four walls. However, I'll admit that not everyone loves them. If you're feeling like you want to bring some interest into your room, and you have a wall that lends itself to being accented, then go for it. I like accent walls in particular for rooms without a ton of architectural detail, where you want to create a little bit of color and texture to spice things up.

In terms of choosing the accent wall, first, you may want to see which of your walls lends itself to being the natural focal point. In a living room, oftentimes it's either the wall that the sofa is facing or the wall behind the sofa. In a bedroom, it's often the wall behind the headboard. In a room with one wall that has most of the windows, that wall will naturally serve as a focal point.

If you don't have a natural focal point in the room, then you've got some options. Play around with how you want the furniture arranged, but also consider the dimensions of the room. For example, if you have a rectangular-shaped room, we usually suggest that you pick one of the shorter walls to be the accent wall. Also, if you have a wall with more doors or large entryways, you may want to avoid that one so that the drama of the accent wall isn't being diminished by a lot of other distracting architectural elements.

Finally, remember that there's more to an accent wall than just paint color. Consider adding texture with wallpaper or adding trim and moldings to add dimension. (I love a good shiplap accent wall, and have a few accent walls in my house with windowpane moldings.)

WHAT SHOULD I DO WITH A ROOM THAT HAS A LOW-LIGHT SITUATION?

I rented a walkup in the West Village one summer during college. My room looked onto an air shaft with the world's tiniest window. It was glorious to be young and living in NYC, but it was also a depressing experience to not ever see even a hint of sunshine while I was in the apartment. Here are some easy ways to work with a room with low light:

Mirrors. This is the one tip that you'll see repeated across designers who deal with low-light situations. It's just science: mirrors help reflect light, which creates the appearance of more light. The best way to use this tip is to hang a mirror directly across from your most prominent natural light source to get maximum reflectiveness.

Don't block the light. Try to make sure you think about light flow in a room. What's light flow? Well, it's simply how light is able to circulate and reflect in your room. So don't block a window with dark and heavy curtains (think light and airy sheers), and consider moving large or heavy feeling furniture pieces that have the potential to block the little light you do get.

Layer lighting. We know that this tip is scattered throughout the book, but it really works! Think about adding a beautiful chandelier, as well as table and floor lamps, throughout the room. You can also talk to an electrician about adding more ceiling lights in general, which tend to create a glow in the space.

Use colors to play up the mood. In rooms that you want to appear more bright, use light and airy wall colors; just make sure to not go too "cool" in your whites, if you don't want the room to appear too dingy. Think about playing with colorful art and accent walls to create some brightness and bring some fun energy into a lower-light room.

I'll admit, though: sometimes I just play into the atmosphere. This is particularly good for basements, where it's not your main living area (so you have lightness elsewhere in the home) but you have a naturally low level of sunlight in the space. In my basement, I tried a creamy white but then ended up paneling the space and painting it a navy blue, and made a bedroom a charcoal color. It created a cozy feeling that made the room's lower light level to feel intentional. Our basement living room is now one of our favorite rooms for watching TV.

HELP! MY LIVING ROOM HAS CURVED WALLS AND/OR WEIRD ANGLES.

Not every room is perfectly symmetrical and shaped like a box, and that's what makes those rooms special. If you have a less typical room shape, you will want to thoughtfully plan your room and really find a way to make those unique spaces work with the room, not against them.

Square off the main area. Most people think you have to use the whole of your living space, but that's actually not true. If you have a room with a strange nook or odd angles, consider finding a focal point and creating a space that doesn't have odd angles. A good example is if you have a living room with two main walls that are parallel to each other but the other walls are not, forming a parallelogram.

Consider effectively creating a rectangular seating area in the middle of the room, with the rug square to the parallel walls to create the space, and the sofa and chairs surrounding that, to create a rectangular space. Yes, this will mean you'll have a little excess space on the perimeter of your seating area, but it'll make the space feel cohesive and cozy.

Consider using some of the extra corners as a good place to put some plants, a sculpture, or tapestry, or even storage—like a bookcase or console.

Separate a larger or long and narrow room into zones. My bedroom is large, but that doesn't make it less awkward. It has a clear area for the bed, but then it has a lot of open space to fill, and even has a large bump-out framed by a lot of windows. The first thing I did was create some blocks for different activities in the room. For example, I have a cozy reading area, where we placed some oversize but modern chairs, a cozy rug, and a coffee table. I have a dressing area, with a dresser and some art and lighting. I even filled in an awkward angle with a full-length mirror and some plants. This helps fill in the space but also prevents the room from feeling too big and awkward.

Lean into the weird. When we collaborated with Keltie Knight on her LA living room (see page 24), we knew we were in for a treat. It was a very unique space, but most interestingly, her living room had curved walls! She really went for it by pairing the curves of the space with her key furniture pieces. She highlighted the fluidity of her walls by acquiring a plush velvet sofa that was also curved and a dramatic brass dome chandelier from Restoration Hardware. To avoid everything feeling too repetitive, she paired all the curves with a live-edge coffee table that brought in some organic contrast with its shape.

The moral of the story? Consider using your awkward areas to your advantage. Highlight your home's idiosyncrasies by echoing the shape in your furniture, and think about playing into the quirks of your home.

CONCLUSION

If you're anything like me, you're exhausted right now. There's a lot to think about when you're designing an entire home, but I promise you, it's easier than you think if you follow some of our guidelines, and it's so worth it. While this book was in its first rounds of editing in 2020, the U.S. declared eight weeks of shelter-in-place. All of a sudden, home became everything to us: our offices, our schools, our movie theaters all in one place. The importance of having a well-designed, comfortable home was underscored in a way that even I was surprised by. As we think about our homes, remember that it's a place of togetherness, it's where we create the memories that we will cherish, and it's where we gather to relax, celebrate, commiserate, and have fun with each other. Isn't that worth the investment?

Brands Named

- Anthropologie
- Apple TV
- Article
- Benjamin Moore Chantilly Lace
- Brooklinen
- CB2
- Design Within Reach
- Diptyque
- IKEA
- Interior Define
- Le Creuset
- Nintendo Wii
- Parachute
- Restoration Hardware
- Serena and Lily
- Sunbrella

Websites Named

- Amazon
- Etsy
- Pinterest
- Target
- Ultraguard
- Wayfair

ACKNOWLEDGMENTS

First and foremost, we want to thank the entire team at Havenly. Countless people put time and effort into helping us pull this book together, and many ideas and learnings in the book were derived from insights developed by our incredibly talented team. In particular we'd like to thank Heather Goerzen, who tirelessly shaped the imagery on these pages, and Shelby Girard, our very first designer and our design guru for life, who taught us so many of the things we know about design. We feel honored to be able to curate their collective wisdom and bring it to the world here. We'd also like to give a shout out to Veronica Collins (our very own Veronicalligator), who taught us so much about how content works hand in hand with our brand, and whose energy contributed so much to this effort.

We'd be remiss if we both didn't thank our families, particularly our Dad, Asok Motayed, for teaching us a love of reading and writing, and our Mom, Saswati Motayed, for first introducing us to the world of home design. We'd also like to send love to our respective husbands, Jason and Chase, who support us in everything we do, and don't even seem to mind when we're up in the middle of the night doing edits.

This book would never have happened if Kristyn Benton at ICM hadn't found us, encouraged us and held our hands every step of the way. Last, but not least, a huge thanks to Dervla Kelly, Lizzie Allen, Lauren Kretzschmar, Andrea Portanova, Dan Myers and the rest of the fantastic team at Ten Speed/Penguin Random House, we're grateful to have a phenomenal crew of talented people supporting us, without whom we would never have seen this come to life.

Lee & Emily

Published in the United States by Ten Speed Press, an imprint of Random House, a division of Penguin Random House LLC, New York.
www.tenspeed.com

Ten Speed Press and the Ten Speed Press colophon are registered trademarks of Penguin Random House LLC.

Library of Congress Cataloging-in-Publication Data

Names: Mayer, Lee, 1982- author. | Motayed, Emily, author.
Title: Design the home you love : practical styling advice to make the most of your
    space / by Lee Mayer and Emily Motayed.
Description: First edition. | New York : Ten Speed Press, an imprint of the
    Crown Publishing Group, a division of Penguin Random House LLC, 2021.
Identifiers: LCCN 2020015451 (print) | LCCN 2020015452 (ebook)
Subjects: LCSH: Interior decoration. | House furnishings.
Classification: LCC TX311 .M3925 2021 (print) | LCC TX311 (ebook) | DDC
    74—dc23
LC record available at https://lccn.loc.gov/2020015451
LC ebook record available at https://lccn.loc.gov/2020015452

Hardcover ISBN: 978-1-9848-5661-6
eBook ISBN: 978-1-9848-5662-3

Printed in China

Editor: Dervla Kelly
Designer: Lizzie Allen | Art director: Emma Campion
Production designers: Faith Hague and Mari Gill
Production manager: Dan Myers
Prepress color managers: Nicholas Patton and Neil Spitkovsky
Copyeditor: Amy Bauman | Proofreader: Rachel Markowitz
Publicist: Lauren Kretzschmar | Marketer: Andrea Portanova
Additional photographs by Kylie Fitts, Christopher Lee, Petra Ford, Anthony Isaac

10 9 8 7 6

First Edition